Letters to Andrew Carnegie

A CENTURY OF PURPOSE,
PROGRESS, AND HOPE

Letters to Andrew Carnegie

A CENTURY OF PURPOSE,
PROGRESS, AND HOPE

CARNEGIE CORPORATION OF NEW YORK
2019

CONTENTS

PREFACE

In 1935, Carnegie Corporation of New York published the *Andrew Carnegie Centenary*, a compilation of speeches given by the leaders of Carnegie institutions, family, and close associates on the occasion of the 100th anniversary of Andrew Carnegie's birth.

Among the many notable contributors in that first volume were Mrs. Louise Carnegie; Nicholas Murray Butler, president of both the Carnegie Endowment for International Peace and Columbia University; and Walter Damrosch, the conductor of the New York Symphony Orchestra whose vision inspired the building of Carnegie Hall. The *Andrew Carnegie Centenary* not only memorialized Mr. Carnegie, but also highlighted the accomplishments of the many organizations he had left in private hands to be administered for the public good.

One of the book's most affecting passages belongs to Henry James, president of the Teachers Insurance and Annuity Association (TIAA), an organization Mr. Carnegie helped establish to support educators in their retirement. "We, who in one capacity or another are serving institutions that Mr. Carnegie founded, know well how far in space and in time this one man's shadow is cast," Mr. James stated. "And we know, too, how often we turn back to him in our thoughts and then find faith and hope as we lay the forward course by reference to his directions." Like all Andrew Carnegie's endeavors — from libraries to peacebuilding organizations — TIAA was established to fill what he saw as a critical societal need.

Andrew Carnegie died on August 11, 1919. To mark this centennial, the leadership of the institutions he founded offer this collection of letters as a tribute to the continuing impact of his philanthropy. Like the earlier volume, this new book is meant as a reflection on a century of effort to achieve Andrew Carnegie's enduring vision. It also constitutes a rededication by the Carnegie family of institutions to their singular mission to achieve "real and permanent good in the world" as they strive to "lay the forward course" into the future.

Vartan Gregorian
President
Carnegie Corporation of New York

Introduction

When my colleagues at Carnegie Corporation of New York asked me to write this introduction, I at first expressed my reservations to Vartan Gregorian, given there were others who, in my opinion, possess greater knowledge of Andrew Carnegie and the myriad disciplines his institutions promote. He countered, however, that I have been both a witness and a participant in upholding Andrew Carnegie's great legacy, and this book would give me the opportunity to formally show my deep and enduring respect and appreciation for the work of our sister institutions.

For the past 25 years, I have been privileged to work at one of Andrew Carnegie's legacy foundations, Carnegie Corporation of New York, and I have witnessed some of the greatest achievements not only of Carnegie Corporation, but of all the institutions founded by Andrew Carnegie. If he were alive today and could see all that his fortune and goodwill have accomplished, I know he would be pleased. Of course his work is not yet finished. Now, 100 years after his death on August 11, 1919, the leadership of the Carnegie institutions who honor and carry on his legacy, and Mr. Carnegie's great-grandson, William Thomson, have written letters to Andrew Carnegie recording their collective achievements, future aspirations, and even some failures, in this singular publication, *Letters to Andrew Carnegie.*

Truth be told, I did not know much about Andrew Carnegie upon starting my job at Carnegie Corporation, but I quickly became an avid student of this great man. The more I read about him, the more I became fascinated with his philanthropic endeavors. In 1901, Andrew Carnegie sold his steel empire to

J.P. Morgan for $480 million (over $14 billion in today's dollars), making Mr. Carnegie the richest man in the world. He had spent down most of his fortune by 1911, and endowed Carnegie Corporation of New York in perpetuity with the remaining $135 million. In 1915, at the age of 80, when asked to state his business — by then fully embracing his new profession as a philanthropist — Carnegie declared: "My business is to do as much good in the world as I can." By the time he died in 1919, he had built more than 2,500 libraries; supported scholarships; and donated to science and research projects, hospitals, concert halls, and museums. He built public bathhouses and parks, and donated more than 7,500 church organs in all. Few projects bear his name, but Andrew Carnegie did establish over 20 Carnegie organizations that today carry out their collective missions of promoting democracy, peace, education, and science, while honoring heroic deeds at the highest, most selfless level.

One story about his giving that Andrew Carnegie happily told many times was the purchase of Pittencrieff Park, a sprawling estate in his hometown of Dunfermline, Scotland, owned by the Hunt family. This was the same Hunt family who had, decades before, banned Thomas Morrison, Sr., Andrew Carnegie's maternal grandfather, and his entire family from ever entering the property. The reason: Mr. Morrison had successfully sued the Hunt family for refusing to grant access to the historical sites in the park. As a result, for one day a year, the park was opened to all members of the public except the Morrisons, the family of the man who had made it possible. A reversal of fortunes forced the Hunts to put the estate up for sale. Andrew Carnegie, by then a very rich man who remembered the decades of petty injustice against his family, bought the entire property and donated it to the people of Dunfermline. Recalling the donation in his autobiography, Mr. Carnegie wrote, "Pittencrieff Glen is the most soul-satisfying public gift I ever made, or ever can make. … This is the crowning mercy of my career! I set it apart from all my other public gifts." To show their gratitude toward its most famous son, the townspeople of Dunfermline later erected a large statue of Andrew Carnegie at the center of the park. Today there is a path leading to the statue that, in 2013, was named "Vartan's Way" in honor of Vartan Gregorian, a leading steward of Andrew Carnegie's philanthropic legacy.

All of these institutions are beneficiaries of Andrew Carnegie's generosity and his largesse, and we stand united, at this centennial moment, in remembering our founder and in saluting each other as we all rededicate ourselves to carrying out the missions, both disparate and intertwined, for which he endowed us.

A number of significant dates in Andrew Carnegie's life have inspired leaders of the organizations he founded to embark on special projects in his memory. Toward the close of the twentieth century, Carnegie Corporation and its sister institutions planned to mark December 10, 2001, the centennial of the day Andrew Carnegie committed himself to philanthropy, with a major celebration. No one could have foreseen the tragedy that would befall our nation, and indeed the world, three months earlier, on September 11, 2001. In the wake of the attacks, the trustees of the Carnegie organizations debated postponing the event. Ultimately, they decided to carry out their plan and "greet the twenty-first century with optimism and determination."

Thus, on December 10, 2001, a new century for the Carnegie institutions had begun.

The Centennial was marked with two resolutions. In the first to be ratified, the institutions jointly rededicated themselves to their founder's missions:

> *All of these institutions are beneficiaries of Andrew Carnegie's generosity*
> *and his largesse, and we stand united, at this centennial moment,*
> *in remembering our founder and in saluting each other as we all*
> *rededicate ourselves to carrying out the missions, both disparate and*
> *intertwined, for which he endowed us. We are the many branches*
> *of the tree that sprang forth from the roots of his extraordinary foresight*
> *and philanthropy. In our missions and our undertakings we embody*
> *the great work of improving the lot of humanity through science,*
> *education, culture, research and philanthropy; through the quest for*
> *peace and the preservation of historical places; and through the*
> *recognition of ordinary people who do extraordinary things. In this*
> *way … the Carnegie organizations assembled here have contributed to*
> *the advancement of modern civilization and to thwarting the forces*
> *of suffering and ignorance.*

In the second resolution, they created the Andrew Carnegie Medal of Philanthropy to be awarded:

> *… to an individual or individuals embodying our founder's vision*
> *of assuring that private wealth serves the public good. …*
> *As the family of institutions who carries on Andrew Carnegie's*
> *legacy, we believe these awards will stand as testimony, before*
> *the international community, to the power of one person to*
> *make a difference and to the enduring belief that individual*
> *freedoms can assure great men and women and great societies.*

Closing the meeting that day, Governor Thomas H. Kean, chairman of Carnegie Corporation of New York's Board of Trustees, who presided over the gathering, declared, "We are not marking an ending, but proclaiming a new beginning for all of us."

Now, 100 years after Andrew Carnegie's death, Vartan Gregorian, the president of Carnegie Corporation, envisioned *Letters to Andrew Carnegie* as a way to commemorate the centennial of this event. This volume, comprising letters to Mr. Carnegie from the heads of the institutions he founded, shares reflections on his lasting influence on each organization. Upholding his philanthropic vision, these institutions continue to research, explore, invent, discover, and disseminate ideas and to instill knowledge and promote peace and democracy, thus improving the lives, security, health, and freedom of people around the world. The letters in this book serve as a testament not only to Carnegie's philanthropic legacy, but also to the partnerships and friendships cultivated among the Carnegie institutions, and to the continuing role each plays in realizing Andrew Carnegie's vision for the future. Our deepest thanks to Joel Rosenthal for sparking the idea for this book when he shared with us a collection of speeches honoring Andrew Carnegie on the centennial of his birth. Thanks, too, to Vartan Gregorian for leading the effort to create this book, for strengthening the bonds between the Carnegie institutions, and for creating opportunities to connect with Andrew Carnegie's descendants. And sincere thanks to William Thomson, Andrew Carnegie's great-grandson, for his very special contribution to this book.

I conclude with a quote from Mr. Carnegie's "The Gospel of Wealth," in a way his own "Letter to Andrew Carnegie," which still serves as a foundational document and continues to inspire philanthropists around the world: "… the man who dies leaving behind him millions of available wealth, which was free for him to administer during life, will pass away 'unwept, unhonored, and unsung,' no matter to what uses he leaves the dross which he cannot take with him. Of such as these the public verdict will then be: 'The man who dies thus rich dies disgraced.'" Mr. Carnegie, you have indeed accomplished the business of doing much good in the world. Your legacy lives on.

Jeanne D'Onofrio
Chief of Staff
Office of the President

Carnegie Hall

Dear Mr. Carnegie,

It is my privilege as the Executive and Artistic Director of Carnegie Hall to commemorate this special anniversary year by reflecting on the transformational impact that your incredible Music Hall has had on the cultural life of New York City, as well as its far-reaching influence on music around the world.

As the Carnegie Hall team enters this beautiful landmark building each day, you are well remembered not only for your love of music, but for the way in which you aspired to ensure the best possible results of whatever you set out to accomplish, your belief in access to education for all, and your commitment to building an enterprise that would be sustainable through the years. Your vision still inspires us today and remains an integral part of our institution's DNA.

Everyone who cares about great music is fortunate that, while sailing to your honeymoon in Scotland, you and your new bride Louise — who sang in the Oratorio Society of New York — crossed paths with one of our city's leading conductors, Walter Damrosch, and that, after much conversation, you agreed to build an ideal hall for concert music in New York. While Midtown in that day was centered around 14th Street, we appreciate that you ignored the critics and had the foresight to place your hall much further uptown, understanding that our growing city would soon stretch beyond its conventional boundaries. Construction of the building progressed remarkably quickly — from start to finish in less than a year. When the Hall's doors opened for the first time on May 5, 1891, you ensured that Russian composer Pyotr Ilyich Tchaikovsky, the most famous musician of the day, was at the center of the

festivities, marking Carnegie Hall from its very beginning as a place where audiences would experience the best in music.

From that moment, Carnegie Hall established itself as a place where music history is made. Over the years, the Hall's renown has been rooted in its stunning acoustics, the beauty of its three concert halls, and its location in New York City. Over the course of more than a century, it has played a central role in elevating the city into one of the world's top cultural capitals.

When the Hall's cornerstone was laid in 1890, you proclaimed, "It is probable that this hall will intertwine itself with the history of our country." This has been true from the start. Since Tchaikovsky first stepped onto its platform, Carnegie Hall has been an irresistible magnet for talent and an aspirational destination for the world's finest artists, all inspired to follow in the footsteps of the greats who appeared before. From Dvořák, Mahler, Bartók, and Bernstein to George Gershwin, Billie Holiday, Benny Goodman, Judy Garland, Count Basie, The Beatles, and Frank Sinatra, pioneering political and social figures along with classical, jazz, and popular music icons have all played a part in placing the Hall in a unique position at the intersection of music performance and social and political discourse.

In your cornerstone speech, you also commented on your desire that "all causes may here find a place." I believe you would be pleased to know, as a venue that was never segregated and always open to all, Carnegie Hall has become a place dedicated to the best of almost every kind of music, and a prominent public forum for such causes as women's suffrage, labor, and civil rights, as well as the home of civic events, rallies, graduations, and community gatherings of almost every kind. In addition, over the last decade, Carnegie Hall festivals have connected cultural institutions citywide to explore some of the most relevant themes of the day through the arts, for example: musical traditions from around the globe; how migration has contributed to America's culture; the turbulent social landscape of the 1960s in the United States; and many more.

As its benefactor, you hoped Carnegie Hall would be embraced by the community, and that, over time, it would stand on its own. When times changed and the city continued to evolve, the Hall came within a hair's breadth of the wrecking ball in 1959. We think you would have been moved to see the remarkable advocacy of the great violinist Isaac Stern, rallying citizens to protect and preserve this incomparable musical gem, grasping what the concert hall would mean to future generations. Purchased by the City of New York in

Facing crumbling infrastructure, peeling paint, and water seeping through the ceiling, the artists and city leaders who made up Carnegie Hall's new board of trustees stepped forward as stewards of the building.

1960 and established as a non-profit organization, Carnegie Hall entered a new phase of its life as a public trust. Facing crumbling infrastructure, peeling paint, and water seeping through the ceiling, the artists and city leaders who made up Carnegie Hall's new board of trustees stepped forward as stewards of the building, eventually raising more than $500 million in capital and endowment funds to restore the Hall to its original glory, transform the outmoded underground recital hall into the fully contemporary Zankel Hall, underpin and expand the Hall's concert presentations and education programming, and gain deserved recognition for Carnegie Hall as a national historic landmark and international center of culture.

Given your strong belief that everyone has the right of access to education, we believe you would appreciate that music education has become central to Carnegie Hall's mission today. The two Studio Towers atop the building, which you originally had constructed to attract artists who would provide rental income to support the Hall, have been renovated into Carnegie Hall's Resnick Education Wing. These beautiful new spaces now ensure that more and more people have the opportunity for music to become a meaningful part of their lives. Complementing the array of performances on the three stages below, innovative music education and social impact programs created by Carnegie Hall's Weill Music Institute — most offered free or at low cost — now fill the building's upper floors with students, educators, young aspiring artists, families, and community members of all ages coming together to make and enjoy music. Through technology and partnerships, these initiatives are increasingly leveraged to reach more than 600,000 people in concert halls, schools, and community settings around the globe.

In the coming years, you can be assured that Carnegie Hall's commitment to the future of music and the role it can play in transforming people's lives will continue to grow — not only with the increasing breadth of programming within its three halls, but far beyond its walls, in ways that even you may not have been able to imagine! In keeping with our role as a leading concert hall of the twenty-first

century, we will continue to advance music education by sharing online resources with partners worldwide; we will enlarge the circle of people who can enjoy our performances by webcasting select performances from Carnegie Hall's stages to music lovers around the globe; and we will share Carnegie Hall's story with more and more people online, including through our digital archival collections, an initiative funded in part by Carnegie Corporation of New York. Although we will soon be reaching many more people beyond our walls than within them, the flame of your extraordinary legacy within Carnegie Hall will always illuminate our work around the globe.

It is with great pleasure that we thank you for your generosity and for all that you contributed personally to enrich the lives of people around the world. We know, as we look to Carnegie Hall's next one hundred years, that its future chapters will be at least as exciting as its illustrious past. The peerless institution you created has an almost unlimited potential to change lives for the better through music, and this will forever remain the inspiration as well as the responsibility of all who serve here.

With all best wishes,
Clive Gillinson
Executive and Artistic Director

Dear Mr. Carnegie,

I wish that it were possible to walk with you through the rooms, the stacks, and the spaces of Carnegie Library of Pittsburgh's Main Library. I can imagine an enlightening conversation in which you share your original vision for the design and I tell you what has changed since you founded this library in 1895. Together we could marvel at the ways in which the building has evolved to accommodate the collections and services we offer today. It would be such an honor to be able to see our library through your eyes.

I know that you would expect our collection of books to have grown significantly since your time. They fill the stacks and spill into spaces that were originally intended for other purposes. We collect and curate wisely, and have done so since the day you opened our library. Our collection reflects both what is current and what is most important to keep from the past for the people of today and for those in the future.

You would likely be amazed but not surprised by the technology that is available to us and the ways in which the Library uses that technology both to manage our work and to connect people with content and resources from all over the world. As it was from the very beginning of Carnegie Library of Pittsburgh, we know that the people of our community need to master new tools and acquire new knowledge in order to meet their goals. Through the years, we have made products and devices available that speed access to information and foster skills proficiency for work, educational, and life success.

I would want to take you out to Pittsburgh neighborhoods to visit our branch libraries. You will find that some of the libraries that you built still stand as vibrant, welcoming anchors in their communities. A few of the original buildings are no longer functioning as libraries or may be gone altogether. In every case, newer buildings serve those communities. Over the years, we have established libraries in neighborhoods beyond those you had originally identified. We now have nineteen locations within the City of Pittsburgh. Nearly all have been renovated, updated, or replaced in the last twenty years.

When we visit, you will still see people reading quietly and children sitting still to listen to a story. You are just as likely to see people working collaboratively on projects, discussing their work, using computers, white boards, and cameras to create or illustrate their ideas. You will hear children singing and laughing, and you can watch them in creative play. You will find spaces reserved just for teenagers, that special stage in life where friendship, aspirations, and an emerging sense of self all come together to shape a promising future. Please be advised that our teen spaces are crowded and noisy, but in a good way. That is how teens learn and grow.

Mr. Carnegie, we must address the best and most important aspect of our Library, and that is the people. By that, I mean the Library staff, the residents of Pittsburgh and Allegheny County whom we serve, and our volunteers, funders, donors, and community partners who support our work. At Carnegie Library of Pittsburgh, we often say the library is something we all do together. It truly takes the collective efforts of our entire community to ensure our  viability and our success. This, Mr. Carnegie, was your original vision as it was reflected in the trust agreement that you established with the City of Pittsburgh so long ago — a document that still serves as the bylaws and operating principles for our Board of Trustees to this day.

In the past few years, we have been fortunate to host naturalization ceremonies at our library. There really is something very fitting in becoming a citizen of our democracy at the public library. I am honored and privileged to address these new citizens each time.

I want to make particular mention of the Library staff. They are as wonderful a group of people as you could ever know, and I would posit that they have always been so throughout the decades of our existence. People who work at the public library have passion — for learning, literacy, literature, and for other people. Early on in the history of the library, an effort was made to hire people who were learned, scholarly, and erudite; who were well versed in history, the arts, literature, and the sciences. Today we still hire for education but we look more for kindness, curiosity, and compassion. We want people who can be interested in whatever someone else is interested in, and who will pursue that interest with a passion until the customer is satisfied.

The public library today is a much more complex organization than it was in 1895. In addition to those who manage and maintain collections and engage people of all ages in literacy and learning, we need staff members who secure our funding, administer our finances, promote our services, oversee our facilities, guide staff support, manage our information technology, and more. You know, Mr. Carnegie, that the library is funded primarily with public dollars. You said yourself that, "unless a community is willing to maintain Public Libraries at the public cost … very little good can be obtained from them." No one will get rich working here. Although we do our best to provide good salaries and benefits, we know people who work at the Library are motivated

by much more than financial gain. We sincerely believe in the mission. We are proud of the words "Free to the People" that are chiseled over our doors.

You would be so gratified to know how important the public library is to so many people. Every day we hear memories and stories that are heartwarming and humbling. People speak fondly of childhood trips to the library with a parent, a sibling, or a friend. They tell us the library was the first place they came when they were new in town and how they found a community here. They share that they borrowed a book that helped them understand they were not alone; others think or feel the same way they do. They say that when they were at the lowest point in their lives, visiting the public library helped them through their troubles. They let us know that with our assistance they got the job, passed the test, won an award, or achieved a goal. At the library they feel they can always be their authentic selves, and that matters. As librarians, we take everyone as they come, and we try to help in the best way that we can.

Mr. Carnegie, I want you to know that you have truly left a legacy that endures. Your work and your story still make a difference. We cite your words and recognize your influence regularly. As an example, in the past few years, we have been fortunate to host naturalization ceremonies at our library. There really is something very fitting in becoming a citizen of our democracy at the public library. I am honored and privileged to address these new citizens each time.

I always tell them about you, Mr. Carnegie, our founder. I tell them you were also an immigrant. I say that you came to this country with your family as a boy from Scotland and settled in Allegheny City, which we now call the North Side. I share that you did not go to school; you had to go right to work to help support your family. I mention a gentleman in town named Colonel James Anderson who had a roomful of books, a veritable library, in his house, and how on Saturdays he would invite the working boys in to select a book to borrow and read for the week. I tell them that you, young Mr. Carnegie, took full advantage of this opportunity, and you credited this reading for your success as you went on to become one of the richest people in the world. When you decided to give back, you built public libraries in our city, region, country, and beyond. You were steadfast in your belief that with access to books and reading and self-directed learning, a person could be anything he or she might want to be. This belief is still core to library services today.

I urge our new citizens to take full advantage of all the organizations and institutions that exist in our country to serve them, including their public library. Of course, they are nervous and excited at this important moment, and may not quite hear it, but each time several people nod and smile when I talk about the library. Sometimes someone will pull out his or her library card to show me, and it grabs my heart.

Mr. Carnegie, I believe that your true legacy is how your particular brand of philanthropy reflects a fundamental faith in people and in our individual and collective desire to do the right thing. Through the institutions and causes you chose to fund, we see evidence of your belief that, given the right support, people will work hard, study, and learn; become better versions of themselves; value science, arts, and culture; aspire to world peace; and risk, even sacrifice, their own lives to save others. People of great wealth today have embraced your conviction that their riches should be put toward health, education, and other causes that benefit humanity. The public libraries you founded are still going strong, ever firm in our belief that access to books and reading and self-directed learning can change lives.

Very sincerely yours,
Mary Frances Cooper
President and Director

Carnegie Museums
of Pittsburgh

Dear Mr. Carnegie,

I am honored to represent Carnegie Museums of Pittsburgh as I report to you on the progress of this, your "palace of culture," which you gifted to Pittsburgh 124 years ago.

It all began, of course, with the construction of your magnificent building — your "monument," as you called it — situated in what is now the Oakland neighborhood of Pittsburgh, Pennsylvania, and home to your beloved library, museums, and music hall. We know from your archived correspondence that you reveled in every detail of the building's design and the many impressive acquisitions of its earliest contents.

At the building's dedication ceremony on November 5, 1895, you spoke with great emotion about the vision you had for your museums. We've decided to use those words as a guide as we consider how the Carnegie Museums of today continue to carry out your noble vision.

"My aspirations take a higher flight," you said to the attentive crowd gathered that day. "Mine be it to have contributed to the enlightenment and the joys of the mind, to the things of the spirit."

Andrew Carnegie opening the Carnegie Institute, known today as Carnegie Museums of Pittsburgh, in November 1895.

We're so proud to report that your high-flying hopes and dreams for your museums have been realized, many times over, and they continue to be celebrated, not only in Pittsburgh but the world over. Most importantly, the museum family you created continues to change lives. You believed museums had the power to transform, by inspiring and challenging the individual. And you were so right!

Physically, the contemporary Carnegie Museums carried out your vision through an ambitious period of growth, beginning in 1974 with the addition of the Sarah Scaife Galleries, which gave Carnegie Museum of Art's constantly growing collections their own elegant space. In 1991, Carnegie Science Center entered the Carnegie Museums fold, serving as a town square of hands-on learning about the science of everyday life, as well as a leader in the STEM learning movement — the application of science, technology, engineering, and math principles; being curious about the world around you, asking questions, and acquiring problem-solving skills. Only three years later, Carnegie Museums again brought something new and irreplaceable to Pittsburgh and the world: The Andy Warhol Museum, the most comprehensive single-artist museum ever built — a fitting tribute to another son of Pittsburgh, who was a graduate of another of your gifts to the city, Carnegie Institute of Technology (known today as Carnegie Mellon University), and who defined what we know as Pop art.

We often wondered what you would think of our decision to more than double our museum family — and, in doing so, more than double our reach — by giving Pittsburgh two new museums in five years. I feel certain you wouldn't have just liked the idea; you would have demanded that it happen!

More recently, the expansion and reimagining of your world-renowned dinosaur hall produced *Dinosaurs in Their Time*, an exhibition truly worthy of its incredible inhabitants, not to mention the first permanent dinosaur exhibition in the world to feature real specimens in scientifically accurate, immersive environments spanning the Age of Dinosaurs. All told, the Carnegie Museum of Natural History today houses 20 galleries that display up to 10,000 artifacts and specimens. And its collection continues to grow as museum scientists undertake fieldwork around the world — from the study of amphibians in Borneo to the unearthing of new dinosaurs in the Antarctic.

(Clockwise from top left) Carnegie Museum of Art, Carnegie Museum of Natural History, The Andy Warhol Museum, and Carnegie Science Center.

All of that physical growth has led to what we believe is a Carnegie Museums family you would still consider "one of the chief satisfactions of my life," as you put it — four diverse museums that lift up individuals and communities through their commitment to educational programming and one-of-a-kind experiences that inspire people of all ages, backgrounds, and interests to explore their world. Carnegie Museums today employs more than 1,000 people, including renowned scientists and curators, greatly enriches the quality of life of the region's residents, and attracts hundreds of thousands of out-of-town visitors each year.

All told, our museums reach 1.5 million people annually, many of them schoolchildren who still look up in wonder at the stately architectural casts and imposing dinosaur skeletons that the people of Pittsburgh marveled at well over a century ago.

It's true that, today, most of those schoolchildren have digital access to seemingly limitless amounts of information and entertainment — the kind of access that the men, women, and children of 1895 Pittsburgh couldn't even dream about. But there's still something profound about seeing Winslow Homer's *The Wreck* or Claude Monet's *Water Lilies* up close and in person. And nothing can replace standing beneath the long, elegant skeleton of your namesake, *Diplodocus carnegii* — the real bones of an animal that roamed Earth more than 160 million years ago.

You were particularly proud to tell your guests at that November 1895 gathering that "already, many casts of the world's masterpieces of sculpture are within these walls. Ultimately, there will be gathered from all parts of the world casts of those objects which take highest rank."

You were speaking of what would become the great Hall of Architecture, completed by you in 1907 after Carnegie Museums' first expansion. That hall continues to engage visitors of all ages with its more than 140 casts of architectural fragments of significant buildings. The Romanesque façade of Saint-Gilles-du-Gard, which was commissioned by you specifically for the Hall of Architecture, is still the breathtaking centerpiece of the collection.

In the decades that followed, scores of museums would rid themselves of their cast collections because of space concerns, and because they felt they no longer had any real value. But we continue to celebrate our architectural casts today. In fact, Carnegie Museum of Art's architectural cast collection is one of only three still in existence; the others are London's Victoria & Albert Museum

and Paris's Cité de l'Architecture et du Patrimoine. We're incredibly proud of this fact. What's more, the museum's curatorial team is committed to finding new ways to make this stunning collection even more relevant to audiences today. In 2017, the museum organized an innovative exhibition titled *Copy + Paste*, which looked back at the history of the hall while also looking forward. With the help of colleagues from neighboring Carnegie Mellon, that exhibition experimented with such new technologies as augmented reality and 3D printing — all with the intent of making the Hall of Architecture accessible and inspiring to future generations.

At that 1895 dedication ceremony, you also spoke of the joy that art brought to your life — and when, as a boy, you "first awoke to the sense of color, and what an awakening it was and has been." I'm sure you would be pleased to know that countless children get the chance to have similar awakenings each year when they visit your museums and participate in classes and camps. Alyssia Lowe, a participant in a workshop that encouraged young people to tell their stories through art, had this to say about her own awakening: "To see all of this in person was a life-changing event that I will be forever grateful for. I learned so much about who I am and what I can and will do in my future."

Clearly, few things excited you quite as much as the far-reaching potential of your Carnegie Museum of Art and what would become the *Carnegie International*, an exhibition that has served as an ongoing survey of contemporary art since 1896 — first American art, and then the art of the world. "There is a great field lying back of us, which it is desirable that some institution should occupy by gathering the earliest masterpieces of American painting from the beginning," you told the crowd that November day. "But the field for which this Gallery is designed begins with the year 1896. From next year we may hope that the Nation will have something worthy of being considered in after years a record from year to year. … If this fond hope be realized, then Pittsburgh will be famous for art as it is now for steel."

Today, the *Carnegie International* is the oldest exhibition of international contemporary art in North America, and the second oldest in the world. Most importantly, it continues to educate and inspire countless audiences, promote

"My aspirations take a higher flight," you said to the attentive crowd gathered that day. "Mine be it to have contributed to the enlightenment and the joys of the mind, to the things of the spirit."

the international understanding of art, support the work of contemporary artists, attract the art world to Pittsburgh, and help build and diversify the Museum of Art's expansive collections.

The 57th edition of this great tradition just ended in March 2019, featuring the contemporary work of 32 international artists. I think you'd find one of the art installations particularly interesting: the work of Tavares Strachan, a Bahamian-born and now New York-based artist. His colorful additions to the exterior of your great building proved to be one of the exhibition's most popular artworks.

"I was just curious about the names they already had on the building, and so I just wanted to think about editing, or adding to that list of names people who might be invisible, or who might not ever end up on a building," Strachan said. So he used multi-colored neon lettering to affix the names of modern-day musicians, social activists, authors, and scientists between names of the likes of Aristotle, Darwin, Leonardo, Mozart. Among the names that he added to the building were Matthew Alexander Henson, a black Arctic explorer who was among the first to reach the North Pole, and Qiu Jin, a feminist poet and revolutionary, who became known as "China's Joan of Arc."

Strachan's addendum to history is emblematic, in a way, of a quite serious effort among contemporary cultural organizations the world over to diversify their collections, their exhibitions, and their programming in order to be more inclusive of the world around them. As a purveyor of ideas, Carnegie Museums takes seriously this need to make all audiences feel welcomed and represented. The *Carnegie International* is just one of numerous examples of how our museums are working towards this important goal.

Without a doubt, for me the words that still resonate most from your November 5, 1895, remarks are these: "No man can become rich without himself enriching others."

Your Carnegie Museums were an incredibly thoughtful, forward-looking gift to a city that, at the time, was known entirely for its grit, not its culture. That was exactly the point: that each of us should have the opportunity to explore unknown worlds, past and present, right where we live, and become better for that exploration. And while you supported your initial dream financially, you fully expected many others to follow suit. And many did — including the Heinz, Mellon, and Buhl families, whose patriarchs were your peers in building our great city. The museum projects they helped make possible include the addition of Museum of Art's Scaife wing and Heinz Architectural Center, and the Science Center's Buhl Planetarium.

An impressive number of individuals and organizations continue to support the four Carnegie Museums generously today. They believe, as you did, in their transformational power. They are true believers in your cause, believers in your legacy — as are the women and men I am so proud to work with in the museum family that still carries your name.

Sincerely yours,
William E. Hunt
Chair, Board of Trustees

Carnegie Mellon University

Dear Mr. Carnegie,

Your last visit here was on October 29, 1914, just three months after the start of World War I — a war you had worked hard, but in vain, to prevent. You and Mrs. Carnegie spent the day with Carnegie Tech students, enjoying their creations in metal and print shops and praising their performances in the just-opened School of Drama. To Carnegie Tech students that day, you were a combination of patron saint, role model, and rock star. You were the Pittsburgh boy who made it bigger than anyone, and they listened intently to your advice: "Don't think so much about money and success; focus instead on using your new knowledge and skill to make a contribution. Make life better for your family, your city, your country, and yourself. You are here to make an impact for good on the world around you."

Andrew Carnegie visits the building site of the Carnegie Technical Schools, which he founded in 1900 for working-class men and women of Pittsburgh to learn practical career skills.

One hundred years after your death, your ideals resonate more than ever.

In 1900, when you decided to create a university of your own, you were committed to establishing a beacon of inclusive opportunity, a technical school to educate the sons and daughters of factory workers. You had a vision for an institution that would serve as an engine of economic development in

Pittsburgh, the city where you made your fortune, one that brought a focus on hands-on learning as well as applied problem solving relevant to the needs of industry. You famously assured the mayor of Pittsburgh, "my heart is in the work" – a phrase that the new school took as its motto and that remains part of our culture to this day.

You might be surprised to learn that the Pittsburgh technical school you founded is ranked among the top research universities of the world, with 19 Nobel Prize winners among its faculty and graduates and more than 112,000 alumni making a profound global impact. Yet despite expansions, reinventions, new names, and new programs and locations on five continents, Carnegie Mellon is, to a remarkable extent, still shaped by your founding vision.

The world you knew in 1900 was on the verge of great change, and your school has had to change too, more than once. In 1905, you had the vision to bring creativity and industry together by establishing the School of Fine and Applied Arts within the Carnegie Technical Schools. (It would become the College of Fine Arts in 1921.) In 1912, the institution changed again to become the Carnegie Institute of Technology, with the power to grant four-year degrees in fields such as applied industry and science. Our willingness to evolve to meet the needs of a changing society continued well into the twentieth century, when Carnegie Tech merged with the Mellon Institute of Industrial Research in 1967 to become Carnegie Mellon University, a comprehensive research institution. Today, in surveying our diverse academic landscape, you would love seeing the scientists, engineers, and practitioners like those who first made Carnegie Tech famous, and you would feel equal affection for the artists, humanists, and social scientists who contribute so much to CMU's intellectual and cultural life.

Pennsylvania's steel industry, the source of your wealth, is far smaller than at its peak, but you'd be excited to know that the city of Pittsburgh is well on its way to leading a significant resurgence in manufacturing — this time using technology to make things in a whole new way. And true to your hopes, CMU is now, more than ever, a generator of fresh economic opportunity for the region. Some of the world's most well-known companies have opened offices and created jobs in the city, drawn by the talent that CMU generates. Indeed, nearly three decades after Pittsburgh was almost written off as a place whose glory days were gone, this city has become a hub for the new economy and a model for other cities. CMU has played a central role in this revival.

In honor of your mother and her belief in education, you made sure that education for women was part of the school's mission from the beginning. You would be delighted to know that today, women make up half of our undergraduate population and represent nearly 50 percent of our first-year classes in both the Tepper School of Business and the School of Computer Science, and 43 percent of the College of Engineering. These percentages are two to three times the national average for women in those fields. And almost from the very beginning, we also welcomed international students — immigrants like you and me. Today, one in five undergraduates and more than half of our graduate students come from outside the United States. Far fewer come from western Pennsylvania these days, which might disappoint but not surprise you, considering CMU's international reputation as well as the economic changes across the globe during the past century.

As you envisioned, CMU remains a strong partner with industry in preparing young people for career opportunities, but more than that, companies frequently engage with us to solve real-world problems and create new knowledge. This started early in our history when pervasive interest in human behavior inspired Carnegie Tech to establish the Division of Applied Psychology in 1916, which helped local businesses place people in the right

jobs. Throughout our history, we have continued to leverage close collaboration with external partners to inspire new innovations in research and education. At the same time, the university supports a thriving entrepreneurial ecosystem, with faculty and students creating dozens of companies of their own every year — more than 300 in the last decade.

You were well known for seeking out the most recent technological innovation to improve business efficiency. You would be amazed at where technology has taken us today, and the leading role your namesake university has played in this journey. In particular, the application of information technology to problems in many fields has been core to our research since the first computer arrived on our campus in 1956. At a time when computers were barely understood, we were among the very first to recognize the power of computing, and we made some big bets. In 1965, we established our department of computer science. In 1979, we founded the first robotics institute at a U.S. university. And in 1988, we announced the first college in the world devoted solely to computer science.

Ours is the model that other universities follow, and the paradigm-shifting advancements developed here have had an immeasurable impact. Today, CMU is a world leader in computer science and artificial intelligence, fields that were pioneered on our campus by legends like Allen Newell, Herb Simon, Alan Perlis, and Raj Reddy. Moreover, throughout the past 50 years, Carnegie Mellon has been at the forefront of innovation in this increasingly information-driven society, creating entirely new fields of inquiry, such as machine learning, transition design, decision science, computational biology, and the science of learning. You would especially appreciate our leadership at the intersection of

"Don't think so much about money and success; focus instead on using your new knowledge and skill to make a contribution. Make life better for your family, your city, your country, and yourself. You are here to make an impact for good on the world around you."

technology and the humanities, with economists, philosophers, and policy analysts studying the effects of these emerging technologies on society and the economy, and what they could mean, positive and negative, for equality of opportunity, liberty, and democracy.

Your school has embraced innovation in its educational approaches while setting new national and international standards, especially when it comes to interdisciplinary exploration. In the 1940s, we redefined engineering education with the Carnegie Plan, which required science and engineering students to take courses in humanities and social sciences to better understand the needs of society. I also think you would have been intrigued by the Graduate School of Industrial Administration that was created in 1949 as a brand-new kind of business school forged from interdisciplinary collaboration between economists, social scientists, and applied mathematicians. This new approach, called management science, reinvented business education for the modern era, and today is reflected in our Tepper School of Business.

Hands-on learning is still central to our educational process, just as you planned. CMU students and faculty continue to make and create at every scale, and our state-of-the-art makerspaces enable remarkable innovation. At the same time, our research and creativity serve to expand our knowledge, provoke our imagination, and push the boundaries of innovation. We are developing robots that can perform heart surgery; innovating ways to produce, store, and use energy more sustainably; building molecules that give materials complex new properties; expanding our understanding of the cosmos; creating new

collaborations in technology, media, art, and design; 3D-printing human organs for transplants; integrating policy, ethics, and business to meet the demands of the future of work; and creating software that triumphs over human poker players at Texas hold 'em. (You would likely not approve of gambling, even by a robot — but as an intellectual accomplishment, you would have to admit it is impressive.) At every step, interdisciplinary collaboration is our foundation; we know we accomplish more by working together.

You were always pleased that Carnegie Tech was a fine arts school, with degree programs in applied design and architecture, art, music, and drama. Artistic achievement has not only continued, it has soared; the fine arts are practiced at CMU at a high professional level, with performances of amazing quality offered every week of the academic year. As innovations and new ideas percolate across our society, we also rely increasingly on the boldness of visual arts, music, and theater to process and understand where we have come from, and to envision where we are going. Arts students and faculty are connecting to the research mission in innovative ways, including collaborations that bridge creative thought and scientific experimentation. And our fine and performing arts graduates collect rich national honors, including Tonys, Emmys, and Oscars. Many of them, including another Pittsburgh Andy — Warhol — have decisively shaped American cultural achievement over the past century.

You would be delighted to see that Carnegie Mellon students still approach their work with passion, intensity, and a spirit of community, both inside and outside the classroom. The libraries, labs, and studios are busy around the clock, and students also contribute to our community by performing more than 200,000 hours of service each year. Student organizations thrive, from performing arts groups to data science clubs to multicultural organizations to buggy racing teams. In your honor, the campus culture embraces all things Scottish: academic gowns are lined in plaid, the school paper is *The Tartan*, and no CMU academic ceremony is complete without the iconic sound of bagpipes. Of course, one of the greatest traditions we've kept in your name is an emphasis on philanthropy, as represented by the Andrew Carnegie Society, a group of generous donors who help to fund scholarships, fuel undergraduate research, and invest in the student experience.

Carnegie Mellon University owns a wonderful life-sized portrait of you in your honorary role as rector of the great University of St. Andrews in Scotland. I am told it was one of your favorite images of yourself, and it now hangs outside my office. Standing in cap and gown, you seem at ease in your academic regalia, the consummate university man — but the truth is, you were never that. Although you had very little formal schooling, all your life you were hungry for learning and you had deep respect for practical knowledge and expertise.

As my faculty colleagues prepare students for careers that have not yet been invented, your bold vision, commitment to inclusion and opportunity, and insistence on pragmatic impact continue to serve as our inspiration. In the knowledge-driven world of 2019, your dream of a school dedicated to innovation, creativity, and the betterment of society has never been more vital and more alive.

When I pass by your portrait at the end of each exciting and fulfilling day of this future you envisioned, I am reminded, sir, that our hearts are still very much in the work.

Sincerely,
Farnam Jahanian
President

Carnegie Trust for the Universities of Scotland

Dear Mr. Carnegie,

In 1901, as the very first step of your avowed mission to give away the recently realised proceeds of the sale of your steel company, you generously endowed to the four universities of Scotland and their students a hugely significant sum. The idea that, one hundred years later, Scotland would be home to fifteen universities, plus a further three institutions of higher education, would have seemed extraordinary to you at that time. Nonetheless, by the end of the twentieth century, that was where we stood. And there is no doubt that this and subsequent progress can be seen as being, in no small part, a result of your benefaction.

In the course of that first century, the Scottish universities, while increasing in number, gained an impressive international reputation for education and research and, on the basis of numerous measures, continue to be regarded as punching significantly above their weight. There is no question that the resources provided through the Carnegie Trust for the Universities of Scotland contributed greatly to this development – particularly in the early days when government funding to universities was very modest. Buildings, libraries, and laboratories carrying the name Carnegie bear testament to just some of the initiatives made possible through the funding you provided.

At the same time, and we know very close to your heart, nearly 70,000 students have been supported in their undergraduate studies, most of whom would not have attended university without the financial assistance that the Trust has provided. Including other grants, such as vacation scholarships, over £14 million has been distributed to students in the Scottish universities since our founding.

Alongside student support, the Trust has contributed to the construction of lecture theatres, libraries, and student residences; funded chairs, lectureships, research fellowships, and PhD scholarships; and awarded research and publication grants – to a total of nearly £50 million.

Andrew Carnegie with James Bryce, Member of Parliament and one of the founding trustees of the Carnegie Trust for the Universities of Scotland.

To summarise, we can report that the overall total of £64 million that, since 1901, has been distributed in grants to the universities of Scotland and their students, when translated into present day values, comes close to £500 million. This remains a pretty good return on your original investment of £2 million. And we are still going strong after 118 years!

Inevitably, much has changed over time, as indeed you expected. Whereas in your day only about one percent of the population went to university, now up to fifty percent undertake higher education studies – an achievement that we are confident you would applaud. This growth in educational opportunities and research activities has had a profound effect on the whole university sector. We have been continually grateful for the foresight and flexibility you emphasised in your original Trust Deed, and which became enshrined in the subsequent Royal Charters, under the most recent version of which we continue to operate. You will be pleased to hear that much of the original wording, as written by you in 1901, remains in our governance documentation.

Besides the more than four-fold increase in the number of higher education institutions in Scotland, and even greater growth in student numbers, the most significant change has been the payment, from public taxation, of student tuition fees. The introduction of government support for students in 1948 saw the beginning of a considerable fall in applications to the Trust under your Clause B expenditure heading: *Tuition Fee Assistance*. Exercising the flexibility afforded us in your Trust Deed, expenditure was shifted towards the more general support of university facilities and staff. The evolution in public funding culminated with free higher education being introduced across the UK in 1962, including the provision of means-tested maintenance grants.

The financial barrier preventing students from attending university, which you hoped to overcome by creating the Trust, was effectively removed, leaving us free to consider other means by which we could deliver that part of your mission. Examples of new student support programs that we have introduced include vacation scholarships permitting undergraduates to undertake summer research projects ahead of their final year of study, and fee bursaries for taught master's degrees.

Coming up to date, and following a few policy oscillations, the Scottish Government (yes, there is such a body nowadays!) is ensuring that tuition fees are paid on behalf of students in Scotland for up to five years of undergraduate study. This leaves the Trust acting in a reserve capacity for those special cases in which students either fall outside the government's eligibility rules or have used their full entitlement. Commonly, we pay tuition fees for students who, for various — often difficult personal — reasons, have had to discontinue their degree studies before restarting later. Sometimes these fresh starts also give students an opportunity to think again about the subject area that best suits them and their career ambitions. We help them to move forward.

The second factor leading a student to seek our assistance to pay their fees can relate to immigrant status. Whilst some students may have completed their high school education in Scotland and lived here for a number of years, they may fall outside the government's funding eligibility. Here we can step in — sometimes supporting the families of asylum seekers (in conjunction with a scholarship from their university). We like to think that your own experience arriving in America at the age of thirteen, keen to seek out opportunities to educate yourself wherever possible, would ensure your enthusiastic support for such a use of the funds you have placed at our disposal.

Another major change over the last century, which may surprise you, has been the expansion of research in universities across the UK. Recognising, as you did, its huge importance for the growth of industry, the development of business, and the advancement of culture and society, government agencies in Scotland, the UK and internationally, as well as industry, now provide large sums of money for research in the Scottish universities. Whereas, when you created our Trust, the funding it could provide made a very significant contribution in this area — leading to the creation of an excellent university research base with an outstanding worldwide reputation — our role has, in many respects, been overtaken by these other funders. Our resources cannot compare with these bodies, but nonetheless, we continue to provide an import-ant function by awarding relatively modest research grants to academics at the earlier stages of their university careers. These grants permit lecturers and research fellows an opportunity to explore new areas of research to the benefit of their own career development and their universities, and often lead to the initiation of important new lines of study.

We also assist the development of research careers through the award of Carnegie PhD Scholarships, which are extremely prestigious and highly competitive. Candidates who receive these awards are hugely talented young people and can be expected to achieve great things. Just one past example is Alexander Todd, who was a Carnegie PhD Scholar 1928 to 1931. He went on to receive the 1957 Nobel Prize in Chemistry and, subsequently, as Baron Todd of Trumpington, became Chancellor of the University of Strathclyde (one of Scotland's "newer" universities). We are also proud to record that John Boyd Orr, who received a series of grants from the Trust from 1907 to 1912 in support of his medical studies at the University of Glasgow, was awarded the Nobel Peace Prize for 1949 — an outcome we are sure you would applaud.

On the subject of successful careers, we frequently quote your invitation to students to repay, should circumstances permit in later life, the grants that they received from the Trust. As you said in your letter to Lord Elgin on 7th June 1901, "I hope the Trustees will gladly welcome such payments, if offered, as this will enable such students, as prefer to do so, to consider the payments made on their account merely as advances which they resolve to repay, if ever in a position to do so." You will be pleased to hear that a total exceeding £600,000 has been paid back to the Trust to date, permitting us to support more students over the years.

In addition, your words, together with the impact that our grants have had on the careers of recipients, have led to a number of large donations, including legacies. These have totalled £2.5 million. Converting all these different types of donations into current-day values leads to an overall total of £7.6 million — a powerful demonstration of the esteem in which your Trust is held. Building on this success, the trustees are keen to attract further financial support in this manner so as to extend the work we can do for the further benefit of both students and the universities in Scotland.

Since 2005, the Trust has been based in a stylish new building — opened by HRH The Princess Royal (Princess Anne) — in your home city of Dunfermline. Our offices look out onto Pittencrieff Park, which you so generously donated for the use of the population of the city. Currently on a shelf inside our office is a thank-you card that we recently received. It is addressed to the trustees and reads:

Andrew Carnegie House, Pittencrieff Park, Dunfermline, Scotland, houses the Carnegie Trust for the Universities of Scotland, the Carnegie Dunfermline Trust, and the Carnegie UK Trust.

> *"I wanted to take the opportunity to express my heartfelt appreciation for your support with my course fees and continued financial assistance. It has made a huge difference to my son and I and allowed me to focus on being a mum and achieving my goals. Thank you will never be enough."*

On the facing page, in a more juvenile script, is written:

> *"Thank you for believing in my Mum".*

We are honoured to be able to join the great number of people who have benefited from your farsighted creation of the Trust in expressing our own thanks.

Yours most sincerely,

Professor Dame Anne Glover, DBE, FRS, PRSE
Chair, Board of Trustees

Professor Andrew Walker, FRSE
Secretary and Treasurer

Carnegie Institution
for Science

Dear Mr. Carnegie,

When you established the Carnegie Institution for Science, you laid a foundation for generations of intellectually fearless researchers whose independence has empowered them to seek — and speak — the truth. For decades, we have appreciated your foresight as we have watched national funding for basic scientific research wax and wane due to political and fiscal considerations. Today, our institutional responsibility to take risks and address crucial problems in novel ways is greater than ever, as Carnegie scientists join our colleagues around the world in the urgent struggle to understand and battle the existential threat of climate change. So, as we confront the overwhelming scale and peril of this crisis, we remember your belief in the power of public education, your steadfast support of discovery science, and your constant advocacy for world peace, and we ask ourselves: What would Andrew Carnegie do?

Your life and work would make you uniquely qualified to provide leadership and to offer warnings. In ways both direct and subtle, the present climate crisis is rooted in the technological revolution that you helped generate. It is inarguable that your vision of an American economy built on steel — and on the coal used to produce that steel — set the world on a course that has led to ever-increasing consumption of coal and petroleum and emission of carbon dioxide. Yet you and the corporate titans who

Meeting of the first board of the Carnegie Institution, January 29, 1902.

Today, as Carnegie Institution researchers seek to unlock the secrets hidden within the stars and planets — including our own Earth — you would challenge us to share our unbridled excitement about science in all its forms, and you would charge us to fling open the doors of every scientific discipline to welcome a diverse, vibrant cohort of scientists that looks like the nation we seek to serve, educate, and inspire.

were your peers — John D. Rockefeller, J.P. Morgan, and Henry Ford — could have had no notion of the massive, unintended environmental consequences of your ambitions. You yourself were an outspoken champion of conservation in your time, speaking out on the need to preserve our nation's forests and to improve the quality of our freshwater resources. You stood alongside President Theodore Roosevelt and pioneering environmentalist Gifford Pinchot at a massive national conference designed to raise awareness of the devastating impacts of industry on our land, water, forests, and air. I have no doubt that, were you with us today, you would be a leading voice in the worldwide call for immediate action to halt our heedless emission of greenhouse gases.

More obliquely, we are grappling with the less tangible legacy of your extraor-dinary success in transforming the face of this nation and the world. In the United States of your childhood, horses drew streetcars down narrow avenues and pulled wagons filled with heavy freight from railroad terminals to shops and factories. With millions of horses at work in municipalities across the

United States and Europe, city leaders were faced with the seemingly intractable problem of providing effective, hygienic disposal of horse manure and horse carcasses. Tens of thousands of human deaths each year were attributed to horse waste in New York alone. As human and horse populations increased, the future livability of horse-powered cities seemed doubtful. Then came automobiles, fueled by (apparently) clean-burning gasoline, along with a powerful new electrical grid. Our cities were transformed within a generation, rendering the "horse problem" obsolete. Is it any wonder that so many people maintain an outsized belief in the power of some as-yet-unknown technology to reverse climate change quickly and painlessly, without any need for change or sacrifice on our parts? Calling on your own experience, you could remind the overly optimistic public that the apparently sudden shift to a new energy economy in your lifetime was founded on many, many years of research and experimentation. You also could make clear that averting the pending climate catastrophe will require massive technological breakthroughs that are more complex, by orders of magnitude, than those considered revolutionary in your lifetime.

As we seek ever more urgently for ways to bring people together to fight climate change, I ponder what you would think about the role of public education in preparing us — or in failing to prepare us — to meet this crisis. It is troubling that so many Americans seem deeply suspicious of the scientific community. Whether we are discussing the safety and efficacy of vaccinations or the terrifying impacts of increasing carbon emissions into the atmosphere, we are countered by anti-science contrarians who question both our methods and our motives. In statehouses and school districts around our country, standard science education has been condemned as a partisan tool, and researchers whose work has been completely discredited continue to be cited as "experts" by those who either truly do not understand scientific discourse or who feign ignorance for their own purposes. We desperately need a strong and trusted voice like your own to speak out on behalf of straightforward science education and to bring a level of rationality to these barbed debates. We also could benefit from your insights into the great value, and the great dangers, of the internet, whose hidden corners provide instant access to junk science and conspiracy theories. In a world in which we can find a self-anointed online expert to buttress almost any position, it is difficult to balance the indisputable good of democratic access to information with the potential harms caused by misinformation — especially misinformation that is disseminated for malicious purposes. As we consider the great legacy of the Carnegie Free Libraries, which made self-directed education accessible for millions of Americans, it would be useful to hear your advice on how we might better equip people to sift fact from fallacy, and how we can best use this extraordinary platform to extend, rather than undermine, your purpose of promoting "the advancement and diffusion of knowledge and understanding."

I am sure that your assessment of the present crisis would not spare scientists, either. When you founded the organization that has evolved into the Carnegie Institution for Science, you purposefully forged powerful links between the worlds of science and politics. At your direction, our first board of trustees included the President of the United States, the President of the Senate, and the Speaker of the House of Representatives, as well as the secretary of the Smithsonian Institution and the president of the National Academy of Sciences. You understood that the revolutionary potential of science can be unleashed only in partnership with government, and with the enthusiastic support of the people. Over the past decades, many of us in the scientific community have grown so tightly focused on our work that we have often neglected our duty to reach out to the larger community. Enthusiastic about our own research and optimistic about its future impacts, we thought we could let our work speak for itself; or, perhaps anxious that laypeople would not support science for its own sake, we withdrew into ivory towers in the hope that we could avoid public scrutiny. In retrospect, we needed your reminder that the human passion for science knows no political party, and that pure science has the power to inspire and unite. When you joined forces with the visionary astrophysicist George Ellery Hale to build the world's most powerful telescopes, you didn't seek to justify your immense investment on pragmatic grounds; although you knew that great science leads ineluctably to great technology, you also understood the sheer inspirational value of reaching ever further toward the stars. Today, as Carnegie Institution researchers seek to unlock the secrets hidden within the stars and planets — including our own Earth — you would challenge us to share our unbridled excitement about science in all its forms, and you would charge us to fling open the doors of every scientific discipline to welcome a diverse, vibrant cohort of scientists that looks like the nation we seek to serve, educate, and inspire.

More than anything else, you would require us to raise our voices about climate change, which is one of the greatest threats to world peace that this planet has ever known. It is terrifying to watch humanity's torpor in the face of global warming, as we turn our heads away from the reality that we may be a few short decades away from a manmade mass-extinction event. In your life, you had no greater priority than peace, and you would have foreseen the coming horror of endless wars sparked by drought, famine, and pestilence. Today you would stand up and demand immediate action from leaders in every sector, calling together elected officials and captains of industry around the world to create a bold, effective plan and then to put that plan into uncompromising action.

I know that you would feel a fierce pride in the Carnegie Institution for Science's leadership in climate science. You would applaud our research on coral reefs, which underscores the importance of these diverse ecosystems, both in terms of the thousands of species of fish and plant life that reefs support and of the millions of human beings whose livelihoods depend on coral fishing and tourism. You would recognize that these fragile coral communities serve as canaries in a coal mine, and you would hasten to warn the world that the devastation of our coral reefs signals our own impending doom.

Coral reef in Hawaii, threatened by human activity and increased sea surface temperatures.

Left: Desert Laboratory scientists driving through Arizona. Right: A maize seedling used in research on crown-root suppression resulting from water scarcity.

You would remind us that one of your earliest investments in science, the Carnegie Desert Botanical Laboratory in Arizona, was created in 1903 to help us understand the important ways in which plants adapt to extreme environments. Your visionary establishment of that pioneering desert laboratory brought together an early community of leading plant scientists who went on to help establish the Ecological Society of America. Today, Carnegie plant researchers are continuing this crucial line of research by investigating the intricate molecular genetic mechanisms that enable plants to sense water availability and survive stressful conditions, such as drought and high salinity. By working to better understand drought response, and to find ways to make plants more resilient, our researchers are proving the enduring value of the mission you set for this institution: "To encourage, in the broadest and most liberal manner, investigation, research, and discovery and the application of knowledge to the improvement of mankind."

But even as you encouraged us in our present work, you would continue to sound the alarm about the perils of increasing temperatures, extreme weather, and rising seas. You would remind us that our Institution's independence gives us both the freedom and the responsibility to speak out about our findings, even when other voices in the scientific community are muted by political opposition and willful denial. You would personally storm the White House and the halls of Congress, reminding our leaders of their duty to support American ingenuity and insisting on the funding levels necessary to conduct unfettered climate research and to develop carbon-free energy sources and reliable, affordable energy storage systems. You would bring scientists and government officials together to craft evidence-based policies that will create effective incentives for utilities and consumers to shift away from dependence on fossil fuels and embrace a new energy future. Through your support and your own example, you would call on us to be fearless, just as you were.

Perhaps most importantly, you would give us hope. Your belief in the power of hope shaped your entire life. As a pragmatist, you would acknowledge the enormity of these challenges, which require us to work together on an international scale and quickly pursue effective scientific energy solutions that will save our planet while we still can. But at the same time, I believe that you would persist in a belief that, as humans, our power to amend equals our power to destroy. You would remind us of the exceptional Carnegie scientists whose brilliance has transformed our understanding of our world, and you would assure us that, when bold and brilliant researchers are faced with an urgent mission, they will rise to meet the challenge and find solutions on an unprecedented scale.

Mr. Carnegie, we know what you would do today, because we remember what you did in your own lifetime. So now we must strive to follow your example, fulfill the mission you set for us, and work with even greater passion and focus to change — and save — the world.

Respectfully,
Eric D. Isaacs
President

Carnegie Foundation

Peace Palace

Dear Mr. Carnegie,

When I entered the magnificent Peace Palace, full of engagement to give it my all to promote world peace, little did I know about how you made this impressive building, a beacon for the world, possible. Once appointed, I quickly learnt more about your remarkable life and your vision. I will not get into too much detail about the holistic nature of your vision on the evolving of humankind towards peace, supported by education and science; on the role of individuals, and more specifically the role of leaders, philanthropists, and heroes; and, eventually, the importance of books and the wisdom they contain for human development. Let me just share with you that I became more and more impressed, and humbled at the same time, since it is now up to us to take your legacy into its second century. The challenges we face are hardly less than during your day.

As I started reading about the origins of the Peace Palace that I have the privilege to manage, together with the Board of the Carnegie Foundation Peace Palace and our nearly 50 colleagues, I came across the deed by which you created the Foundation for the purpose of, in your words, "establishing and maintaining in perpetuity … [a] Temple of Peace." You considered the creation of the Permanent Court of Arbitration inside this Palace "the most important step forward of a worldwide humanitarian character which has ever been taken by the joint Powers, as it must ultimately banish war." Your analysis was so true. But a century later, we are not there yet.

So I regularly look back to your words as a source of inspiration. Given your ideas on education and peace, you insisted that a standard library of international law be based at the Peace Palace, too. You established that this Peace

Palace Library should also be maintained in perpetuity, and committed the Dutch government to that end.

Even with your strong belief in technology, you might not believe how a technology that could not be foreseen in your lifetime currently impacts this same library a century beyond its conception. In our day and age, the sharing of information primarily takes place through what you would probably see as a virtual reality, a global web of machines connected both by cables and wireless, giving access to the most diverse sources of information to people all around the world who can afford the technology and the tools.

OUR ANGEL OF PEACE

Andrew Carnegie depicted by illustrator Charles J. Budd as the angel of the international peace movement.

This technology is considered by some a reason why this library would now become redundant. Those who, together with you, believe in the importance of the book, and understand the work of lawyers and academics, realise that books will always be the primary source for sharing knowledge and insights, even more so for the judges and the arbitrators who have to study all relevant resources to develop and underpin their awards. Therefore, no matter what form a book may take in the future, we struggle peacefully but diligently to maintain this crucial facility, the knowledge infrastructure you created for promoting peace through law.

To date, we are working hard every day to promote world peace and banish war. Yet even after terrible carnage in the past century, we still experience warfare on our planet, and we even see tensions rising again 100 years after you left us. Powers do not act so jointly at present. We sometimes experience feelings of despair, as you did when you were deeply troubled and disappointed during the last years of your life, as the Great War broke out after the Peace Palace opened its doors, and the spirit of idealism and hope quickly faded. But it never disappeared.

You lived to see the Armistice, and you may have hoped that lessons would be drawn: such wars never again. Lessons were learnt indeed, and shortly after you passed away, international powers were effectively joined when the League of Nations was established in 1920 to work towards world peace.

The nations recognised the wisdom that prevailed in the era in which you facilitated the erection of the Peace Palace: to promote peace through law. In order to settle conflicts peacefully, the League of Nations decided to add the instrument of jurisdiction to the instrument of arbitration. A second court was installed: the Permanent International Court of Justice. Of course, the first president of the Carnegie Foundation, Mr. van Karnebeek, with whom you opened its doors, was happy to also host this court at the Palace. With international arbitration and jurisdiction, the pathways for peace were laid, and they led to the Peace Palace.

His successor, Mr. Cort van der Linden, wholeheartedly approved of another idea that was born during the Hague Peace Conferences when the first court was initiated: international law as the means to settle conflicts peacefully should be studied and taught as well. Education in peace through law – how well would that notion fit your vision? An academy for international law was to be initiated, and it is Dutch Nobel Peace Prize laureate Tobias Asser to whom we must give credit. He, together with your Carnegie Endowment for International Peace based in Washington, D.C., established The Hague Academy of International Law, and made sure this academy would also be based at the Peace Palace. Thus, the learning infrastructure for peace through law was available as well at the heart of your legacy.

It was a real pleasure, in my second capacity as Treasurer of this Academy, to allow for another program. In 2019, in addition to the renowned summer courses, a new course was started: winter courses in both public and private international law. As of this year, 1,000 bright young students are educated annually as lawyers and diplomats to work towards peaceful relations between states. Your League of Peace, as you called it in your Rectorial address at St. Andrews, is expanding every year.

Incredible as it may seem, war did happen again. The Great War would later be labeled the First World War, as mankind experienced a Second World War some 20 years later, not even halfway through the twentieth century. Could men treat men even worse than during the Great War? Yes, men could. And, unfortunately, it turns out in various places of the world that men still do.

Given its lack of success, after the Second World War the League of Nations was dissolved, and was replaced by another worldwide intergovernmental organisation for cooperation towards peace: the United Nations. Once again, it was decided that the principal judicial body for peaceful settlement of conflicts between states should be based here, at the Peace Palace: the International Court of Justice, a principal organ mentioned in the Charter of the United Nations, now also called the World Court.

It was during this period, after the Second World War ended, that idealism was on the rise again. Human rights for all men and women were even declared as a legal basis for human advancement. Since then, international law has developed tremendously as an invaluable source to settle conflicts peacefully in all kinds of areas. There are global conventions on children's rights and cultural rights; conventions for international commerce; and for health, labour, and social rights. That is deeply satisfying and encouraging. Grotius would have been proud, and I guess you, too.

In order to make peace, more hearings and events take place at the Peace Palace than ever before. Your appeal to the reason of men has been heard. "Law not war" is the motto on a bench recently placed outside the Peace Palace.

We have hosted so many cases in which conflicts have been dealt with successfully. And we don't even know how many battles have been prevented here, but our courts have dealt with the big issues of every decade. We are grateful for every human life saved because of cases settled peacefully at the Peace Palace.

In essence, since you initiated the Carnegie Foundation Peace Palace, we are here to make peace. It's in our genes. A century beyond our founding, we still facilitate peace through law successfully. And we are adding peace through dialogue.

As a consequence of the many cases that are taking place currently, and because older, possibly hazardous materials used in building the Peace Palace should be replaced, renovation is needed to meet current and future demands. This renovation forces us to address fundamental questions: is the host country still committed to recognising and supporting the Carnegie Foundation? If not, what should our role be? What should our strategy be? You encouraged your heirs to act as we see fit. But I would have loved to have you as a sparring partner to deal with these questions.

In all honesty, we did not do everything right during the last century. Unlike fellow Carnegie institutions, we have not kept a financial buffer for maintaining and developing the Peace Palace. Instead, after the budget you so graciously provided for the building of the Peace Palace was exhausted, we relied on the commitment of the Kingdom of the Netherlands. The Dutch government has generously supported our cause for many decades. We recently realised that this dependence entails risks with a view to our mission and our position. We have become vulnerable. So we have to reach out to the likes of you to join our cause and continue the quest for peace together. Will there be an Andrew Carnegie in our time to finance world peace through law, including sustaining the Peace Palace?

As we are acquiring new skills to develop partnerships for peace, we are fortunate to have various Carnegie institutions with complementary missions with

whom to exchange experiences and views. We owe it to the current President of Carnegie Corporation of New York, Vartan Gregorian, that he brought your institutions together again. It is great to experience how the family of Carnegie institutions is with us on our joint mission. When I was in New York for the very first time, meeting colleagues from throughout the world at the amazing Carnegie Hall, I was excited not just to attend the wonderful concert there, but also to meet these great minds and learn about so many impressive initiatives covering the whole breadth of your legacy.

Following a spontaneous plea to join hands in promoting peace, we are taking your legacy to the next level by cooperating more intensely. Just last year we held the very first Carnegie PeaceBuilding Conversations in your Peace Palace. It was inspiring. We launched partnerships for peace, and received wide support to organise dialogues with all kinds of partners to address the root causes of conflicts. Our job will remain the prevention of warfare, carnage, and the loss of human lives. And we do so with many more partners now.

You once said that the peaceful development of nations is their most profitable policy. You will no doubt be happy to learn about the most recent joint initiative of nations. The United Nations has agreed on the Sustainable Development Goals — specific goals to end poverty, hunger, and inequality. There are ambitious plans to enhance education, public health, and sustainable production and consumption. This program is probably by far the most ambitious global program to eradicate root causes of conflicts and develop new avenues toward peace.

We at the Peace Palace focus on a specific goal from this program: peace, justice, and stronger institutions. That is our core business. We are going to facilitate dialogues to promote stronger international institutions to reach these important goals.

For us here in The Hague, now the legal capital of the world, and, as home to the Peace Palace, the international city of peace and justice, it is an honour to follow in your footsteps and try to deliver peace and justice in our day and age. Yet we realise that arbitration and jurisdiction are crucial, but not sufficient. We need to add mediation and dialogue as instruments to settle complex issues peacefully and structurally, so we are laying the foundations for pathways to peace for the century ahead of us.

In essence, since you initiated the Carnegie Foundation Peace Palace, we are here to make peace. It's in our genes. A century beyond our founding, we still facilitate peace through law successfully. And we are adding peace through dialogue. Together with the members of the Carnegie family of institutions and other partners, we create and support great events at a unique location in the world. This is how we bring people together and inspire them to make a change in as many human lives as possible. And we aim to develop more and more partnerships to work together towards world peace.

Thanks to you, Mr. Carnegie, we provide and maintain a tangible place of hope. We facilitate peace in action every day.

You believed that the world takes on a brighter radiance from the day the Temple of Peace opens its doors. We take pride in providing this ray of light to the people. There is hope for the entire world; peace is doable.

With warm regards,
Erik de Baedts
Director

Carnegie Hero Fund Commission

Dear Mr. Carnegie,

It is with great pride that I write you on this 115th anniversary of the first meeting of the Hero Fund Commission. I am pleased to report that this most venerable institution, which you considered your own child, created to serve and celebrate the better angels of mankind, has endured and thrived. You once referred to the Hero Fund as the "noblest fund in the world." After giving more than 10,000 Carnegie Medals for heroism, and nearly $41 million in support for heroes and dependents, our work to honor the true heroes of our society goes on, having proven time and again the noble truths of your insights and the enduring value of your gift.

Beyond the medals and the support that you demanded for heroes and kin so that they "not suffer," the work of the Hero Fund has unraveled the mysteries of the acts and actors impacting our society, as well as the hearts of those who have struggled, overcome, and endured by elevating the value of another's life beyond their own. We have seen that, in all cases, as you seemed to fully understand over a hundred years ago, the hope that has come to those in peril, in the faces of strangers and friends, has been as the presence of angels. Whether lives were saved, or lost, or changed, the hero has imparted hope to the hopeless. Heroes can be considered saviors in a sense for all of us who have witnessed what they did for others, often for strangers. This you recognized early on in the person of "young Hunter" of Dunfermline, and in those who braved the fire and smoke of the Harwick mine. It still exists today in the hearts and minds of the rescuers and victims who have locked eyes in fearsome, and often final, moments.

After giving more than 10,000 Carnegie Medals for heroism, and nearly $41 million in support for heroes and dependents, our work to honor the true heroes of our society goes on, having proven time and again the noble truths of your insights and the enduring value of your gift.

Every one of the Carnegie heroes the fund has recognized personifies that invaluable, God-given trait that you cherished most, and we cherish still: simply that they loved another enough to risk, and in many cases sacrifice, their own lives to try to save them. As purveyors of selflessness, hope, and equality, they represent the possibility for a more peaceful world if, as an ideal, their actions are taken into the hearts of the many, who then do likewise by putting others first.

The fund has provided much-needed support for disabled heroes and for those from whom heroes were taken away, many times far too soon, as a result of their selflessness. As you had hoped, there have been many "exceptional children" for whom the fund has made "exceptional education" a reality. It has soothed the wounds these heroes bear, both visible and unseen. And in all it has done, the fund continues to herald the selfless acts of the heroes among us, for our time and for future generations.

You once said that "the whole idea" of your Hero Fund was contained in the poem "In the Time of Peace" by your good friend Richard Watson Gilder. Its beautiful words ring as true now as they did more than a century ago:

> *A civic hero, in the calm realm of laws,*
> *Did that which suddenly drew a world's applause;*
> *And one to the pest his lithe young body gave*
> *That he a thousand thousand lives might save.*

Coffins hold victims of an explosion in Pennsylvania's 200-foot-deep Harwick Mine, January 1904. Two men died in a failed rescue attempt, inspiring Andrew Carnegie to create the Hero Fund.

Andrew Carnegie's great-granddaughter, Linda T. Hills, left, shakes the hand of Carnegie Hero number 10,000, Vickie Tillman, who rescued a police officer from assault in Baton Rouge, Louisiana.

We rejoice in all of the good that you have done these many years through your gift of the Hero Fund Commission and those hero funds that followed and still thrive. As we look forward to the future heroes yet to join the rolls of honor, we can only offer thanks and hope that your words to the fund's first president in 1905 yet ring true: "You have made a start, and there is to be no finish. It goes on forever." And if it takes forever to find the one millionth "civic hero" and reach the time of peace you dreamed of, I hope and expect that the fund will press on until he or she is found and recognized. For as you knew and taught us, peace will start in the heart of someone who decides to gift it to another in desperate need of it, then build as the many spread it to the world, equally desperate, one heart at a time.

This is my pledge, on behalf of the devoted staff and board of the Hero Fund Commission, who are proud to continue this great work in your name. What you have done has indeed drawn, as Gilder noted, the "world's applause" for those you called "true heroes of civilization."

Respectfully,
Eric P. Zahren
President

Carnegie Dunfermline Trust

Carnegie Hero Fund Trust

Dear Mr. Carnegie,

"To bring more of sweetness and light; that the child of my native town, looking back in after years will feel that … life has been made happier and better. If this be the fruit of your labours you will have succeeded; if not you will have failed."

You wrote these words 116 years ago in your letter from Skibo, founding our Trust, and in this year of the centenary of your death, we will now attempt to reply, laying out how we have indeed tried to succeed.

There cannot be many trusts and foundations which received such clear guidelines as those contained in your three-page letter to us, or many that would turn so willingly to the words of their founder for their current reference points. Yet so it is in our case. Your letter told us to experiment, to be pioneers, to not be afraid of making mistakes, and, in that staggeringly forward-looking and trusting statement, to "try many things freely, but discard just as freely."

How right you were. Needs change, social mores change, and economic environments fluctuate. But poverty is still with us, children still need opportunity and encouragement, older populations face social disconnection, and environmental choices impact on us all.

When we started out, we followed your lead in providing buildings (your name still remains synonymous with libraries). We bought and built children's clinics, children's homes, swimming baths, institutes for both men and women, and recreational, sports, crafts, music, and drama facilities for all. But buildings are costly to run and, with the introduction of national health and welfare services

The cottage in Dunfermline, Scotland, where Andrew Carnegie was born in 1835 and lived with his family until they emigrated to the United States in 1848.

Pittencrieff Park welcomes children of all ages. Its largest play area was installed in 2003 to celebrate the Carnegie Dunfermline Trust's centenary.

in the UK at the end of the 1940s, our ownership of these buildings ceased. Instead, we have moved into direct grant giving, facilitation, partnership projects, and an ethos of punching above our weight. We use your name to engage interest and commitment in pursuit of common agendas based, as ever, on the fundamental principles of need. We hope you would approve.

We have also taken liberties with the interpretation of the "child of your native town." Greater inclusion and shifting educational and economic boundaries have broadened our reach, whilst we still give something special to your local child. In the last couple of years alone there has been a 55% increase in assisting disadvantaged school children, and a growing total of over 4,000 pupils a year enabled to participate in sport. True to "trying many things freely," we support pilot and start-up projects in the hope they will grow and flourish, but not conditional on success as a prerequisite for support.

Also in your all-encompassing letter, you identified Pittencrieff Park as fundamental to our organization's existence. Your pride in its purchase, and our subsequent stewardship, have been constants in our identity. Your wish to see experimentation and development of this magnificent and historic urban green space has led to controversy, debate, financial challenges, and, ultimately, the encapsulation of what green spaces in an urban environment represent. I believe you would appreciate the passion that the park has engendered and perhaps some of the irony that, whilst in 1904 Patrick Geddes' ambitious proposals for the park were rejected by trustees, they are now seen as innovative and relevant, and they form the basis of international study. By degrees, we are

"To bring more of sweetness and light; that the child of my native town, looking back in after years will feel that … life has been made happier and better. If this be the fruit of your labours you will have succeeded; if not you will have failed."

working towards your goal of a recreation space for the people. The Glen Pavilion, new café, and fully inclusive play parks, together with all the open spaces, are nationally recognised and fully used and appreciated all year round. The mansion house, with its double link to Pittsburgh through yourself and John Forbes, is now in the spotlight of opportunity.

In 1908, you added the British-based Hero Fund to our responsibilities. In contrast to our more local work, the Hero Fund takes us across the whole of the UK, Ireland, and Channel Isles. You said the Hero Fund movement was your "ain bairn" (own child), something special and personal to your beliefs. You had already founded the Hero Fund Commission in Pittsburgh, but only we started with a beautifully inscribed Roll of Honour, which today bears moving witness to the nearly 7,000 individuals recognised. Sadly, the majority of these inscriptions are posthumous and, whilst the nature of incidents has changed somewhat with the times, the consistent element of selfless humanity remains throughout. The ongoing support provided to families through the Hero Fund has meant that contact has been maintained, in some cases, for over sixty years — a practice we are proud to continue.

During your lifetime, your wife, Louise, had purchased the cottage in Dunfermline where you were born, to ensure the preservation of its significance. After 1919, she provided the funding to build the art deco hall which, together with the cottage, now make up the Andrew Carnegie Birthplace Museum. Like you, she did not hesitate in her belief that our trustees would

A display in the Andrew Carnegie Birthplace Museum highlights places and events from Andrew Carnegie's life.

manage this area of work, completing our tripartite responsibilities that continue today.

Louise wanted us to tell your story, providing an example of what success can look like, as well as the impact of your international philanthropy, and how others might be encouraged to follow in your footsteps. For some decades we did not value the role of the museum and its potential worldwide voice as we might have, but the establishment of the Carnegie Medal of Philanthropy changed all of that. The greater awareness of the combined voice of all the Carnegie institutions has prompted the museum to revisit the ways in which it tells your story. Your valuing of education, peace, science, entrepreneurship, economic development, and so much more is now conveyed in ways relevant to all ages. Perhaps most significant of all is your living, breathing, and influential philanthropic legacy, one hundred years after your death.

You once said, "There is little success where there is little laughter." Fun and interactive engagement are powerful tools for sharing timeless messages and fresh ideas. As part of the many events of this centenary, your diplodocus replica from London journeyed to Glasgow, providing us with a topical and humorous platform to illustrate so much of your legacy — the shared assembling of a bright red Dippy the Dinosaur in the Birthplace Museum from over 35,000 pieces of Lego. We are certain you would have enjoyed being part of this collective design challenge.

Finally, toward the end of your life, you commissioned a beautiful window from Tiffany Studios in New York as a memorial to your family, to be installed in Dunfermline's historic Abbey. Your reaction when the Abbey authorities rejected the window as not being religious enough was not recorded, but the window then embarked on an eventful and itinerant life, being stored for some years under your baths in Dunfermline, then in the new Carnegie Hall, and, finally, here in our headquarters when they were built in 2007. In what seems a most fitting end to the first centenary of your legacy and the beginning of the next, your wishes were fulfilled in August 2019, when the window was installed in the location you chose.

A Tiffany stained-glass window commissioned by Andrew Carnegie as a family memorial was installed in Dunfermline Abbey as he intended, 100 years after his death.

Have we succeeded? Maybe not always in the ways you anticipated or the ways we would have wished; but we have tried, and, in your own words, we hope you will be "well assured" that we will continue to try to the best of our ability.

Your Trustees of
Carnegie Dunfermline and Hero Fund Trusts

Carnegie Rescuers Foundation (Switzerland)

Dear Mr. Carnegie,

Inspired by a mining accident in Pittsburgh, 1904, in which a miner and an engineer, in spite of great danger, attempted to save the lives of numerous buried people before making the ultimate sacrifice themselves, you founded your first Hero Fund in the United States to give recognition to lifesavers. These events seem to have made such an impression on you and Mrs. Carnegie that you set up similar lifesaver foundations in the UK and Europe in the following years.

Thanks to your initiative and your generosity, the Swiss Federal Council established a foundation in Switzerland in 1912. Its purpose, as you wrote in your Deed of Trust, is to "place people who, whilst pursing peaceful endeavours, have injured themselves during a heroic effort to save human life, in a somewhat better financial situation than before, and to continue such support until they are fit to work again. In the case of death, provision will be made for the widow and any children; specifically, for the widow until her remarriage, and for any children until they reach working age."

Since the foundation's inception, 8,577 lifesavers have been recognised in Switzerland, and over 3.2 million Swiss francs have been paid out by way of pensions and one-time financial contributions.

Much has changed over the course of time, and you will no doubt be interested to know what important developments have eventuated in Switzerland since your foundation was established, and whether the foundation you initiated is still able to meet its objectives.

An important step in the development of our country was the introduction, in 1948, of old-age and survivors' insurance, in effect Switzerland's state-run pension system, and, in 1960, a disability insurance program. These programs have improved the financial circumstances of heroes who were injured during rescues, as well as the dependents of those who died during rescues. In addition to this government support, emerging private and occupational accident insurance as well as non-occupational accident insurance have led to a gradual reduction in the number of pension payments by the foundation.

Rescue services have also undergone changes over the last 100 years. Whilst rescues in the past were carried out predominantly by people on the scene and a limited number of professional helpers, the number of trained rescuers has increased enormously today. This change has not only taken place across professional rescue organisations for land, sea, and air-based rescues, but also across the voluntary rescuer sector. The Scout, Samaritan, and other organisations that emerged during your time and in the wake of the First World War and the Spanish flu pandemic not only spread first-aid knowledge widely among the population, but also led to the establishment of an extensive network of potential rescuers.

A lot has also changed in the rationale for rescues. Today's training sessions and courses for first responders stress that rescuers should not endanger their own lives during a lifesaving operation, but must take appropriate precautions during the rescue process. In line with this, the ways in which rescues are carried out have changed over the years.

Mr. Carnegie, you will probably be asking yourself whether the number of awards is also decreasing proportionately, and whether your foundation is gradually losing its raison d'être. To give you an answer to this question, I would like to briefly mention a case where an award was conferred by your Swiss foundation.

The scene: Zurich-Stadelhofen railway station, Tuesday afternoon, 16 December, 2014. Senat Iseni hears security guards yelling and notices that they are running after a drunken man. Suddenly, the man enters the platform and stumbles — just as a train approaches. Responding instantly, Senat Iseni jumps down onto the track and, with all his strength, pulls the drunken man back onto the platform again. Witnesses later told the rescuer that he himself had only been able to pull his foot clear of the train at the last second. It was something he was not aware of; he only acted.

Senat Iseni received the Hero Medal for risking his life to rescue a drunken man who had fallen onto the railroad track.

69

Despite these inhibiting factors, we are, fortunately, continuing to experience people's selfless acts directed at rescuing others. This requires bravery and civil courage. The recognition of such acts serves us and our descendants as a model for a humane society.

This case illustrates vividly that a lifesaver does not always have the necessary time to consider whether saving a fellow human being could cost his or her own life. In a split second, a rescuer may have to make a life-changing decision: rendering help may endanger one's own life, but if no help is given another person may die.

Although, in retrospect, many people would know how to respond, it has to be said that only a few act courageously and decisively. Many people who would have been able to help intentionally look the other way. Even worse, they might watch the accident spellbound and even hinder the helpers in their work.

Are there any reasons for this? Was such behaviour also common in your day? Is it perhaps a fear of doing something wrong that prevents many people from intervening? Today, this is what we know and learn in first-aid courses: the worst thing one can do after someone has been injured is to do nothing. Perhaps potential rescuers' fear of being made liable for any mistreatments, or prosecuted for substantial damage claims, plays a role in this reticence to act. Certainly a lot has changed here since your time.

Despite these inhibiting factors, we are, fortunately, continuing to experience people's selfless acts directed at rescuing others. This requires bravery and civil courage. The recognition of such acts serves us and our descendants as a model for a humane society.

In our foundation, we consequently believe that your initiative has not only set important developments in train, but also that the recognition of lifesavers remains equally valid today as in your time, for rescuers themselves as well as for all of us, and highlights important examples of praiseworthy behaviour.

We therefore continue to remain grateful today that you and Mrs. Carnegie drew conclusions from a personal experience that continue to remind us now, more than 100 years after your death, of what constitutes the core of a humanitarian society: civil courage and a shared sense of community.

Daniel Biedermann
Board Member

Carnegiestiftelsen

SWEDISH CARNEGIE HERO FUND

Dear Mr. Carnegie,

In 1911, you wrote to the Swedish king and asked if Sweden could accept a gift of US $230,000 in order to establish a foundation with the aim of awarding civil heroes. The king, of course, accepted your generous gift, and the foundation Carnegiestiftelsen was established according to your wishes.

In 1912, the first awards were given and, up until today, 2,399 heroes have received awards. In the beginning of the twentieth century, the rescues were, for example, from small wooden boats in stormy weather, saving sailors whose ships had hit rocks, or rescuing people from drowning or from fires. Today, the heroic acts are largely the same with regard to incidents of drowning and fires, yet a bit different. We have safer rescue boats, and the fire brigade can be called earlier because of our popular cellphones. Now we present awards more often when the hero has saved people from a burning car, or has helped someone who has been attacked in a dangerous way.

Our latest case involved a young man, 23 years of age, who saved a man from drowning after his car had gone into the water by a ferry berth. It was in February 2018, around 10:00 PM, dark and cold both in the air and in the water. Our hero had gotten out of his car, which was the only one waiting for the ferry, when he suddenly heard a cry for help. He realized that a car had gone over the quay and into the water, and he saw a man who had succeeded in getting out of his car but did not have the strength to swim. Our hero jumped into the water, swam to the man and took him to a cliff, but could not pull him out of the water because he was heavy and the cliff was slippery. The rescuer's cellphone did not work because it had gotten wet, but he found a working cellphone in the man's pocket and used it to make an emergency call. In the meantime, he realized that the ferry was on its way and they both could be drawn under due to the current and the waves caused by the ferry. He told the man at the emergency center about their situation, who managed to call the ferry and stop it before it was too late. Both men were saved by a rescue team after about twenty minutes in the cold water, hanging onto the small cliff.

In the early days of Carnegiestiftelsen, there was almost no social welfare in Sweden, and the foundation often gave support to families of deceased heroes who had died saving, or trying to save, someone. The foundation also gave money to younger heroes for their education, or to help establish a home. Today we have a welfare system in Sweden, so there is no need for such

Our hero jumped into the water, swam to the man and took him to a cliff, but could not pull him out of the water because he was heavy and the cliff was slippery. The rescuer's cellphone did not work because it had gotten wet, but he found a working cellphone in the man's pocket and used it to make an emergency call. … Both men were saved by a rescue team after spending about twenty minutes in the cold water, hanging onto the small cliff.

support from our foundation. The awardees get a certificate, a watch with an inscription, and a sum of money.

In earlier decades, the foundation awarded quite a few heroes every year. Life was harder at that time. Nowadays we find fewer heroes because life is, in many ways, safer.

In 1993 the board found that there was enough money to support research with the aim of saving lives when accidents occur, and the statutes were changed accordingly. The foundation has so far given 6,874,300 Swedish kronor (US $742,365) to such research.

There are so many people in our country who are thankful for your generous gift, which has helped heroes have a better life.

The board of Carnegiestiftelsen has, in recent years, had the opportunity to meet representatives from other foundations established by gifts from you, and we have been able to exchange experiences. We have made many good friends in the Carnegie family.

Thanks a lot for your generosity! It has made a tremendous difference for Swedish heroes. We who work with Carnegiestiftelsen look forward to the years ahead, fulfilling your mission in accordance with your initial letter to the Swedish king.

Yours sincerely,
Ann-Christine Lindeblad
Chairman of the Board

Fondazione Carnegie per gli Atti di Eroismo

ITALIAN CARNEGIE HERO FUND

Dear Mr. Carnegie,

I have often gone back and thought of you – about your clear and decisive work, appreciated equally by heads of state and the wider community, for the promotion of world peace and heroic acts aimed at achieving peace.

When? Definitely during the Commission's meetings, which I have been a part of for 24 years, and where I am time and again faced with the question of whether we can continue to have full impact with funds that do not permit us to thoroughly fulfill our duties and, in a deaf society, our attempts to represent difficulties that have existed for too many years. The answer I give myself is always the same: the path you, Mr. Carnegie, have shown continues to be valid and relevant, and your tenacity and generosity inspire us yet. The theme of peace has been, and still is, spoken about extensively; it is a dream that we all have deep inside, but which has always remained a grand illusion.

The Emperor Augustus had the Ara Pacis built in 9 B.C. because he was convinced that the known world was heading towards a long period of peace. By then, Rome was the sole dominant power without the need to expand further, while the bordering nations or tribes feared it and often asked to be incorporated into the Empire. We know very well that just a few years later, Augustus was forced to move legions to quell rebellions or ward off invaders.

In the seventeenth century, after the bloody invasion of South America and the Christianization of the indigenous people, the Jesuits, who were very powerful at the time, decided to establish "reductions" aimed at peacefully converting the local people in those far lands. This plan stemmed from the conviction that such communities would easily become Christian civilizations similar to those in Europe, but free of their vices and flaws. In reality, conversions were achieved by force, many locals fled, justice gradually moved away from the word of the Gospel, and conflict among villages increased.

When the Berlin Wall fell in 1989, world peace was celebrated, and the media euphorically claimed, "History is over." We soon realized that a balance had been broken within the areas of influence of the two superpowers, giving way to fragile crisis areas and local wars with unpredictable developments.

Even the trust put into the League of Nations, which was established to prevent World War II, turned to disillusionment. When a dictator has a plan to claim territories, the one language he understands is force. Diplomatic negotiation is only interpreted as a sign of weakness to the bitter end.

In nature, life is asserted through competition, selection, and the law of the strongest; when stillness takes over, so does death. We have to acknowledge that humanity has never strayed too far from this primordial principle. It seems that recent major achievements that vastly improved the possibility of exchanging information have not increased awareness of the uselessness of conflict and the value of human life. Even religions, with their teachings on life, have been, and still are, tumultuous at times. Moral laws may be impeccable, but they are managed by humanity, and when man convinces himself that he is legitimately entitled to interpret the divine word, he acquires a confidence that prompts him to act fanatically and dangerously.

You were well aware of human limits and flaws; however, you were able to maintain your love for your neighbour and your conviction that we should work towards a peaceful world, even one small step at a time.

In our work, we consistently see this tendency towards the good, even if our community has not yet learned how to properly emphasize acts of generosity and altruism; these always take second place to selfishness and criminality. I believe that cultural education is the basis of true progress, and that nonviolence is the fundamental theme that must guide our every activity. It is not civil for example, for thousands of police officers to risk their integrity in order to prevent protesters from damaging public or private property, under whatever pretense, or in order to keep rivals apart.

Numerous acts of heroism continue to occur, and are often thrilling. Over the century, recognition of our institution has greatly improved, yet gaps remain. In Italy, very little is known of our organization and its philanthropic purpose. Up until World War II, the large amount of capital available was, in itself, a source of publicity, as were the cash prizes and scholarships for orphans, which were an unusual type of aid in our society. With almost total depreciation of our assets after the war, the Commission's operations were drastically reduced. We have not "thrown in the towel" because we are convinced that we have a noble task, as you have shown us, and because, occasionally, we have received help that allowed us to survive, such as now from the Carnegie Hero Funds World Committee. Moreover, I do not believe that we have yet done everything possible to increase our assets, and I feel we have a duty to find new ways to obtain funding as well as to improve visibility.

We have moved in this direction, and we intend to solicit banks to sponsor us by ensuring them adequate recognition. At the same time, we will bring awareness to the Ministry of the Interior, which provides us with an office, and to other public institutions, suggesting that medals or diplomas awarded to their employees be presented during dignified public ceremonies.

With a touch of optimism and trust in the good inside each one of us, we hope to breach the wall of indifference surrounding us.

We continue to believe in your work and in the progressive betterment of humanity; it is to your teachings that we owe our motivation to move ahead.

Gaetano Melini
President

Stichting Carnegie Heldenfonds

DUTCH CARNEGIE HERO FUND

Dear Mr. Carnegie,

We are honoured to be a part of the family of Carnegie institutions. The relevance of the Dutch Carnegie Hero Fund has not diminished. Today, polarization throughout the world, as well as in the Netherlands, is growing. Humanity needs humanity. Heroes show the impact of being human toward one another.

The Dutch Carnegie Hero Fund is just a small member of the family, yet proud of being the offspring of that family. Its role in this part of the world has grown. In a manner of speaking, it has become a senior adult now, well aware of its purpose and yet searching for the best way in which to be part of creating a better world. Just as you tried to do, we aspire to leave a better world behind.

In 2015, the first National Hero Day took place in our country. We started this initiative to try to get a message across to Dutch society: Look at the heroes amongst us and see how they have acted as co-owners of society.

In the Netherlands, heroes are rewarded on a local level. Most of the time the mayor gives the medal in front of the local community. The aim of the National Hero Day is underlining the importance of people who act when it is needed.

Our purpose is to let this event grow as a relevant annual moment, with media coverage through which the significance is broadly recognized. We believe our society needs it, and we feel indebted to you for our being placed in The Hague, the city of peace and justice, the city with the Peace Palace, International Court of Justice, and various pillars of your "Temple of Peace."

Today, polarization through-
out the world, as well as in
the Netherlands, is growing.
Humanity needs humanity.
Heroes show the impact
of being human toward
one another.

Three Dutch heroes received medals on the first National Hero Day, October 7, 2015, for rescuing a woman from her car as it was sinking in a canal in Amsterdam. Rescuers (left to right) Sander Schönhuth, Gijsbert Paul Vroom, and Martin Snel; Utrecht Mayor Jan van Zanen, who presented the medals; and Jaap Smit, Dutch Hero Fund president.

We don't want to do it alone. After starting as a platform with other awarding organizations, the National Hero Day is becoming more and more a real national phenomenon. All organizations (royal medals, Royal Society for the Rescue of Drowning People, police, fire brigade, military) share the same objectives — giving thanks to heroes and letting others know.

One man can make a difference. You did, many years ago. Many, many people are involved in the various aspects of your legacy.

The board of trustees of the Carnegie Hero Fund of The Kingdom of the Netherlands wishes to express its gratitude for being part of the Carnegie Hero Funds World Committee, and we are very thankful for all support given by the Carnegie Corporation of New York.

Yours sincerely,
Jaap Smit, MSc
President

Boi A.J. Jongejan, MD
Vice President

Carnegie Foundation for the Advancement of Teaching

Dear Mr. Carnegie,

On this, the 100th anniversary of your passing, I am honored, as the ninth President of the Carnegie Foundation for the Advancement of Teaching, to take a moment to reflect upon your legacy and impact in the field of education and to ruminate on the challenges that still lie ahead.

It is with a sense of awe and humility that I approach this task, recalling the words of Nicholas Murray Butler, former President of Columbia University, on what would have been your 100th birthday: "What greater responsibility could any one of us bear than to have been asked by him, or by those whom he asked, to assume a share in the conservation of these forces which he set in motion, in their direction and guidance for human betterment through the next generation?" We are not stewards simply of the funds, but also of the ideals, and it is the ideals that continuously inspire and challenge us.

First and foremost, Mr. Carnegie, I continue to be inspired by your belief that teaching can and should be a dignified profession. You founded the Carnegie Foundation for the Advancement of Teaching with the specific goal, as stated in our charter by the United States Congress, to "encourage, uphold and dignify the profession of the teacher." Since its inception, the Foundation has kept this value in mind, manifesting it in our work to elevate standards for higher education, strengthen preparation for the profession, honor the scholarship of teaching, and, in the Foundation's current work, bring teachers and researchers into more productive collaborations to address longstanding inequities in educational outcomes from pre-K to post-secondary.

Secondly, you believed strongly in the innate capability of persons and the capacity of institutions to learn and to improve. The Foundation has spent the majority of its more than 100 years convening leaders across the education landscape with the aim of making our educational institutions more efficient, more effective, and more student-centered. From the Flexner Report, to the recommendations from the Carnegie Commission on Higher Education, to the establishment of the Carnegie Classifications, to our current work on using improvement science principles and organizing improvement networks, there is a long history at the Foundation of convening educational leaders around improving our educational institutions.

Lastly and most importantly, Mr. Carnegie, I continue to be inspired by your belief in the power of education to transform lives. In "The Gospel of Wealth," you recall with "devotional gratitude" how Colonel James Anderson of Allegheny would open his library to the children of Pittsburgh. You, your brother, and Henry Phipps would attend every Saturday to exchange books. You never forgot this example of openness and generosity, and you believed that one of the best uses of your wealth was to fund universities, libraries, museums, and parks — palaces for the people, where anyone can have access to the knowledge, beauty, creativity, and noble spirit contained within these open spaces. You considered it your duty, even a privilege, to gift educational institutions to communities around the world, and these communities continue to reap the benefits. You recognized that a productive and convivial democratic society rests on the education of its citizens. Unless more had access to the kinds of learning opportunities that had been afforded you, a free, civil, and open society could not endure.

Having grown up in a blue-collar working-class family, the only child on either side of my family to attend college, I know personally the power of education — the intellectual world that it opens as well as the social and economic opportunities that it affords. Having worked in the field of education for over forty years, I have seen again and again how education can ennoble and enrich students' lives, but I have also seen how quality education continues to be denied to far too many of our nation's children.

Theirs is most noble work: to inspire, to shape, and to help each child have a meaningful personal life and become a productive contributor to that ongoing great experiment of democracy in America.

So yes, Mr. Carnegie, having access to institutions of knowledge and culture not only brings value into our own lives, it also strengthens the social fabric of our communities. But today we need to do more than just create access. Our aspirations for our education system have increased dramatically over the past four decades. We now aspire to achieve quality educational outcomes for every child. We use these words so effortlessly now — every student succeeds — that we can easily underappreciate how ambitious these goals really are. Never before have we challenged educational systems in this way.

We often hear stories like yours and mine, where people of modest means succeed through some combination of family support, intellect, grit, and, often, that special teacher who touched their lives. But we should not let our personal accounts blind us to the great tragedy of the countless numbers of children who continue to be denied opportunity for a better life by virtue of the community they may have been born into or their family life circumstances. We must expect more from our education systems.

In order to achieve the ambitious goals that we now hold, to educate every child well, we need to work in very different ways. This may well sound strange to you, Mr. Carnegie, as Frederick Taylor was a contemporary of yours and greatly influenced the evolution of the industrial workplace, including your steel mills. As significant as his ideas were in fueling the industrial revolution, the seeds of great human debasement were also embedded within them. Taylor assumed that he knew best how to organize work, and that laborers should simply follow his directions. Workers were, in essence, replaceable parts. He wanted their labor, not their minds; nor did he attend much to their dignity as human persons. It took W. Edwards Deming, some forty years later, to challenge this thinking. Deming argued that if all you ask of your workers is their labor, your organization is throwing away 90 percent of its social intelligence for problem solving. Deming's insights are especially important now, as the educative tasks in our schools and colleges have become more complex, and the organization necessary to carry out this work more complex as well. To reach a new effectiveness frontier requires a social organization well beyond the mechanical formulations of an earlier era. Moreover, we live in a time of extraordinary, sustained, and rapid change. Our educational institutions not only need to get better, they need to learn how to continue to get better, as our society will continue to demand even more changes over the years ahead.

Education today is a vast institutional enterprise involving millions of educators and over 100,000 different contexts in which students regularly interact with teachers around subject matter. Making every one of those contexts work every day for every teacher and child is a daunting task. Moreover, there is no simple "new idea" waiting in the wings to solve this problem. The solution won't be found in just adopting some new curriculum, or adding another program or some new web-based apps, regardless of how promising any of these might be. In truth, these are all just parts, albeit potentially valuable parts, but their power remains inert unless we focus on how these various parts become more productively integrated into the fabric of our educational organizations. In short, we confront a systems improvement problem. How can we get our educational institutions to work better and more reliably every day for every child in every context in which students are educated? There is no *deus ex machina* to save us. Rather, we need to roll up our sleeves and take up the sustained and sometimes tedious tasks of continuously improving how our educational institutions can create more value reliably for all who walk through their doors every day.

Today we confront a growing chasm between rising aspirations as to what we want from our schools, and what they can routinely accomplish. Realistically, we have no strategy to achieve our rising aspirations, whether it be all children reading by grade 3, all children career and college ready by the end of high school, or all new teachers succeeding in educating their students.

Comprehending this reality demands a fundamental shift in how we think and act toward educational systems improvement. Much practical learning occurs every day as people engage in their work. Numerous fields have become much more productive by acknowledging this natural inclination to learn by doing, and then building on it in deliberate, systematic ways. Moreover, the problems we now seek to solve are too complex to lend themselves to broad-based solutions by individuals or institutions working in isolation. Rather, we need to join in deliberately structured improvement networks that attend to practical problem solving.

This means getting down into the micro details of how our educational systems actually work, and how any proposed set of changes is supposed to lead to improved outcomes. It means using evidence to guide the development, revision, and continued fine-tuning of how tools, processes, work roles, and relationships might better interact to produce the outcomes we seek.

In addition, it is important, but not sufficient, to know that something can work (i.e., what we now call "evidence-based" and store in the What Works Clearinghouse). We also need to build the practical know-how necessary to generate quality outcomes reliably under diverse and different conditions. This means paying explicit attention to variability in performance, and questioning what works for whom and under what set of conditions.

In the past, we have relied on a select group of people to design interventions and establish policies, and then those actually doing the work — teachers, principals, and education leaders — are cast as followers of these directives. In contrast, effective organizations today, across many different sectors, draw on W. Edwards Deming's insights and actively engage those involved in the work who are central to its improvement.

Rather than assume that some external experts already know the answer to improving schools, we need to listen to what students, teachers, and their families are experiencing and how they are making sense of the social world in which they live. We need to understand better what is and is not working for them and why this may be so. As Danielle Allen reminds us in her book, *Our Declaration: A Reading of the Declaration of Independence in Defense of Equality*, respect for the voice of others — the right to be heard — is the most basic expression of the concept of equality. So it is incumbent on those who have power to use their power to truly listen to the voices of those we seek to engage, who are most dependent on our good efforts for their success.

As large and complex as this problem is, I am also convinced that we can learn better and faster. Most recently, I saw this in action at our sixth annual Summit on Improvement in Education. Over 1,700 people from around the country and around the globe gathered together for three days of workshops, presentations, and conversations, all aiming to improve educational effectiveness and reduce inequities in educational outcomes. It was a thrilling event where participants felt inspired, empowered, and enabled to make a difference in their local contexts. I think you would have been proud to have this event

A meeting in the early days of the Carnegie Foundation for the Advancement of Teaching, attended solely by men.

carry your name; proud that more than 100 years after your passing, thousands of educators were working together to dignify the profession of teaching, to make schools and colleges more effective, and to make progress toward our aim of educating well every child.

So here in the twenty-first century, we continue to be enlivened by and to advance upon your inspiration to do all things that encourage, uphold, and dignify the profession of teaching and to improve the institutions where it occurs. Theirs is most noble work: to inspire, to shape, and to help each child have a meaningful personal life and become a productive contributor to that ongoing great experiment of democracy in America.

In closing, I thank you for your great gifts, Mr. Carnegie. Both the investments themselves and the spirit with which those gifts were given continue to inspire and challenge all of us who are charged to be good stewards to your legacy.

Sincerely,

Anthony S. Bryk

President

Participants in a recent Carnegie Summit included a diverse group of practitioners, researchers, thought leaders, and others at the cutting edge of education.

Carnegie Endowment for
International Peace

———◆———

Dear Mr. Carnegie,

When you established the Carnegie Endowment for International Peace, you charged its board with the constant renewal of the Endowment's mission. As you wrote, "Lines of future action cannot be wisely laid down … let my Trustees therefore ask themselves from time to time, from age to age, how they can best help man in his glorious ascent onward and upward."

You founded the Endowment at a critical historical juncture. In many corners, optimism about the world's interconnected future was reaching a crescendo — just as the foundations of international order that prevailed in the nineteenth century were beginning to crack. Hopes for a more peaceful world seemed close to realization — yet catastrophic war and disorder loomed. The last great surge of the Industrial Revolution was transforming the global economy, bringing with it a host of opportunities and challenges. It was against this backdrop that you challenged the Endowment to promote new actions and ideas that could bend trendlines in a more peaceful direction.

Today we find ourselves at another transformational moment — a moment again defined by cataclysmic threats and unimaginable opportunities. The past century has seen unspeakable horrors, as well as extraordinary progress for peace and the welfare of humankind. But the optimism that overflowed after the end of the Cold War is rapidly giving way to foreboding currents: the return of great power competition; a new technological revolution that is upending how we live, work, and fight; a shift in the world's economic and military center of gravity, from West to East; and growing tensions between open and closed societies, with nationalism and authoritarianism resurgent.

93

Walls are going up faster than they are coming down. Democracy's march has slowed, and even reversed, and the prospect of international law and cooperation is withering on the vine. The tailwinds of globalization — those same forces that you saw shrinking our world into "a neighborhood in constant and instantaneous communication" more than a century ago — have transformed into powerful headwinds, and trendlines once again seem headed towards massively destabilizing collisions.

Like the international system itself, the marketplace of ideas is more diffuse, crowded, competitive, and contested than ever before. Decisionmakers were once starved for information, but today they are drowning in it. Where there was once a small number of trusted brokers of insight and analysis, today's policy actors now have to navigate a cacophony of voices across countless platforms, with greater skepticism than ever about their reliability, credibility, and independence. Today's policy discourse is more polarized and divisive, and civil society is under growing suspicion and scrutiny.

That is precisely why now is the time to answer your charge anew. The Endowment has changed a great deal over the past century. Today we are a global institution, with more than 140 scholars spread across 20 countries and six global centers in Beirut, Beijing, Brussels, Moscow, New Delhi, and Washington, D.C. We aim to do more work on and in Africa and Latin America in the years ahead. But even as we adapt to new realities, we nevertheless hold steadfast to our core values: global reach and perspective at a time of heightened insularity; unassailable independence at a time of hyperpolarization; and disciplined, strategic focus on the most consequential issues facing our world at a time when punditry is drowning out serious public discourse.

In 1912, Carnegie's Board of Trustees opened a permanent European Bureau in Paris to act as a communications center between Europe and North America.

94

Opening of the Carnegie-Tsinghua Center for Global Policy in Beijing, April 14, 2010.

Harvey V. Fineberg Chair Thomas Carothers (left) meets with Gilbert M. Khadiagala (center) and Niranjan Sahoo (right), members of Carnegie's Rising Democracies Network, in Barcelona.

We continue to believe, as you did, that we have "no party where Peace is concerned." We represent no national, political, or private interest, nor do we promote an institutional policy agenda. We simply believe that the essential prerequisites to understanding the drivers shaping a changing world — let alone addressing the challenges they pose — are rigorous analysis and innovative solutions informed by ground-truths, enriched by diverse regional and ideological perspectives, and directed smartly to key decisionmakers and the public square.

To rise to the challenge before us, we've continued to evolve and adapt, focusing on the most significant forces shaping the emerging order, and concentrating our efforts where our global platform has the most to offer.

With on-the-ground expertise in key regions, we provide sophisticated analyses of the societal, economic, security, and political forces fueling competition and conflict, bringing our global network together to find pathways to conflict mitigation and resolution. We publish in multiple languages and engage with a variety of players who have a stake in outcomes, as well as the ability to shape them. Ours is a world in which governments remain essential to questions of war and peace, but their monopoly on power, access, and influence is not what it once was. That makes the work of peace ever more complex, even as it allows more of our fellow citizens to contribute to its achievement.

Ours is a world in which governments remain essential to questions of war and peace, but their monopoly on power, access, and influence is not what it once was. That makes the work of peace ever more complex, even as it allows more of our fellow citizens to contribute to its achievement.

With a mix of world-class economists and strategists, we are helping executives from situation rooms to boardrooms rethink the critical intersection of economics and national security — ensuring that our international relations contribute to the renewal of our own societies. I remain convinced that while foreign policy begins at home, it must end there, too — in better jobs, more security, and a cleaner climate. In the United States, that does not mean casting aside the enlightened self-interest that has defined American leadership at its best, but it does mean we need to think more imaginatively and do a better job bridging the disconnect between card-carrying members of the Washington establishment and American citizens.

Together with governments and other organizations around the globe, we are working to strengthen and sharpen the ways in which outside actors can more effectively support civil societies and democracies that are under unprecedented strain. In too many places, the compacts between state and society are far too brittle, and ideas on how to enliven them are far too stale. The challenge is only becoming more urgent, as authoritarian regimes increasingly feel the wind in their sails.

And, finally, we are working to help the development of international norms and rules of the road catch up to the pace of technological innovation — seeking to maximize the promise of new technologies while minimizing their disruptions. You would be amazed at the technological progress we've made in the instruments of both peace and war. Since the advent of the nuclear age, we've mostly managed to keep the genie in the bottle, but that task is going to be far more challenging in the digital age, making the Endowment's work that much more important.

The most fateful error in international politics is failure of imagination. It was failure of imagination that preceded the wars that engulfed our world in the last century. If we are to finally rid ourselves of war, what you rightly termed "the foulest blot upon our civilization," we will need to overcome that failure of imagination as well as the failure of action.

It is the awesome responsibility of this Endowment, and all those charged with executing its mission, to meet this moment with the energy, wisdom, and determination that it demands. And it is our hope that your legacy will continue to inspire other philanthropists for peace. We need them more than ever.

Sincerely,
Bill Burns
President

Carnegie Corporation of New York

Dear Mr. Carnegie,

In your autobiography, you wrote, "I intend to tell my story, not as one posturing before the public, but as in the midst of my own people and friends, tried and true, to whom I can speak with the utmost freedom." That is also my intent in this letter. Every day, when I walk into my office, I see your statue and your portrait. Every once in a while I imagine that you are looking back at me, and I hope you realize that Carnegie Corporation of New York still strives to uphold your mission "to promote the advancement and diffusion of knowledge and understanding." As a historian, I'm fully aware that I have inherited a great mantle of responsibility. After all, I am the second immigrant to preside over Carnegie Corporation. You, of course, were the first. Growing up in a relatively poor family in Tabriz, Iran, I never dared to dream that I would someday be among your successors.

In retrospect, our worlds, though distant, were not so far apart. Our formative years were shaped by strong women, yours by your devoted mother; mine by my beloved grandmother, Voski Mirzaian. Although she was illiterate, my grandmother knew the importance of education, and she instilled that belief in me. You and I both loved books as children. I understood instinctively what you meant when you wrote about your youth in Pittsburgh, Pennsylvania, and the way books and libraries "opened windows" for you, as if they were letting light into a dark room.

Just as you had Colonel Anderson to loan you books, I too knew kind individuals who gave me access to their libraries and thereby opened new worlds. In Tabriz, I read noncirculating books at the Armenian diocesan library. In fact,

I volunteered to be a book-shelver there at age twelve, precisely for that privilege. Like you, I loved to read. And my world expanded as I read translations of Persian, Russian, French, and German literature. Occasionally, I read books about "self-made men," where I came across your name for the first time.

Another source of light for me was the private library that belonged to Miss Boodakian, the sister of a local bank president, who lived in a large house in a wealthy neighborhood. She generously lent me her precious leather-bound books, one at a time. There was also a stationery store in town, where I found lighter reading material, like detective stories featuring the master of disguise, Arsène Lupin. With shrewdness worthy of Monsieur Lupin, the store owner divided his books into three parts, which he rented out to customers, charging each time, and tripling his profit.

Later in life, when I learned that you were the father of the modern public library system, I was filled with gratitude. Thanks to you, millions of individuals have been able to read books and discover new worlds of their own. Yet you did it in such a way that the public took ownership of their libraries, providing the building only if the community agreed to establish the library's collections and support the cost of its operations. You were wise to create new partnerships between the private and public sectors, seeking to empower others rather than to control them.

A Justice of the United States Supreme Court, Clarence Thomas, once spoke about his gratitude to you and to Carnegie Corporation for building a library for African-Americans in Savannah, Georgia. During his childhood, this library was, to him, "an outlet on a whole other world." Justice Thomas reminisced, "I would walk into the Carnegie Library, and I would see the pictures of Booker T. [Washington] and pictures of Frederick Douglass, and I would read. Did I dream that I would be on the Supreme Court? No, but I dreamt that there was a world out there that was worth pursuing."

Subsequently, when we met, Justice Thomas sent me a thank-you note to express his gratitude, describing the Carnegie library as a "sanctuary."
I felt exactly as he did, finding a sanctuary in one library after another −

Of course, there are at present many forms of inequality in the world, and virulent ethnic and racial tensions still persist in defiance of the Enlightenment principles you believed in. But Carnegie Corporation still maintains, as you did, that people and nations can live together in peace, and adjudicate their differences through arbitration.

the Collège Arménien in Beirut, the library of Stanford University, and the New York Public Library.

Yet you did not open windows only through your libraries, you also opened them by establishing institutions devoted to honoring heroism, strengthening education, and promoting international peace. You were ingenious at finding appropriate purposes and fitting names for this commonwealth of organizations, all united by the goal of doing "real and permanent good in this world," as you put it in your essay, "The Gospel of Wealth." I am happy to report that today your vision and mission are still carried out by Carnegie Corporation of New York, as well as its sister entities. Those institutions have endured, unlike so much of the ephemera in our modern world. You made sure that our missions were relevant, and that we were well organized and well funded. Moreover, you wisely gave those Carnegie entities and their leadership the freedom and the funds to adapt, to meet new challenges, and to pursue new vistas. Today, all these institutions have one thing in common: they embody your optimism and perpetual dynamism.

How fortunate Carnegie Corporation is that you gave a great deal of thought to your philanthropy. It still has both purpose and coherence. We have also always been fortunate to be guided by excellent governing boards, which have included distinguished diplomats, financiers, political leaders, educators, authors, journalists, generals, and others. They share your commitment to the mission of the Corporation. The stability and continuity of Carnegie Corporation is reflected in the number of presidents we have had — only twelve in 108 years. Each president who succeeded you arrived at a different transitional moment, and made an important impact. Your charter provided the Corporation with both flexibility and clear goals, allowing us to be at the forefront of nearly every major issue.

Today, international peace remains a pillar of our work. In keeping with your vision for a world without war, the Corporation continues to champion peaceful negotiation, arbitration, and diplomacy. We supported negotiations to reduce weaponry and strengthen global security, resulting in pacts such as the Nunn-Lugar Act. By establishing the Cooperative Threat Reduction Program (CTR), the Act helped states of the former Soviet Union effectively safeguard and dismantle their enormous stockpiles of nuclear, chemical, and biological weapons. We also promoted U.S. engagement with countries and regions during challenging periods in bilateral relationships, encouraging diplomacy and sustaining engagement when official governmental relations were limited.

U.S. Senators Sam Nunn (left) and Richard Lugar (right) at the Nunn-Lugar Cooperative Threat Reduction Symposium in December 2012, where President Obama spoke on the 20th anniversary of the CTR program.

We continue to fund official efforts to reduce tensions and build understanding among countries, through the United Nations and, perhaps most effectively, by encouraging Track II negotiations, a creative unofficial diplomatic channel that allows nations to find common ground. Your belief that education cultivates peace led us to establish research centers where scientists and intellectuals from rival countries learn from each other, fostering trust and fellowship.

We helped build and sustain the peacebuilding field in Africa, reinvigorated the study of China and Russia in American universities, and funded Middle East and Islamic Studies for almost twenty years. Of course, there are at present many forms of inequality in the world, and virulent ethnic and racial tensions still persist in defiance of the Enlightenment principles you believed in. But Carnegie Corporation still maintains, as you did, that people and nations can live together in peace, and adjudicate their differences through arbitration.

In our own nation, we remain committed to helping immigrants become a part of the civic fabric of the United States because, like you, we believe that, "along with the freedom to pursue wealth and happiness, the greatest gift the American Republic has to bestow is citizenship." In 2001, the Corporation launched its current immigrant integration program, which encourages immigrants to become citizens, and focuses on improving current federal immigration policies as well as supporting pro-immigrant and refugee policies at the national and state levels. In addition, every year we publish a list of "Great Immigrants" with your photo at the center, saluting your legacy along with the contributions of the millions of other immigrants who have made, and continue to make, our nation strong and vibrant. Understanding that enlightened citizenship is the foundation of our democracy, we also support civics education, funding a national campaign on the need to restore civics and history in school curricula.

We continue to believe that Americans should think not just of themselves, but of the nation; not just of the rights but also of the responsibilities of citizenship. Since the early 1980s, we have consistently funded nonpartisan voter registration and turnout efforts as well as voter protection efforts for new citizens from immigrant backgrounds. We are proud of our long history in support of voting and voting rights, and we work to ensure that all those who are eligible to vote have the opportunity to cast a ballot.

Through the decades, we have acted on your belief in equal education as the right of all citizens. In 1921, the National Urban League, a civil rights organization dedicated to economic empowerment and social justice, received its first major foundation grant from Carnegie Corporation. In the 1960s, the Earl

Warren Legal Training Program (the educational affiliate of the NAACP Legal Defense and Educational Fund) and the Law Students Civil Rights Research Council received more than $3.4 million to address a critical shortage of black lawyers, particularly in the South.

Your generosity and your faith in education were reflected in your support for universities and your work on behalf of the professoriate (including the early funding of what would become TIAA). Carnegie Corporation has played a major role in education from early childhood to graduate school here in your adopted homeland, in your native Scotland, and around the world. When I think of all that has been done in your name to support the education of women – grants for fellowships in the humanities, financial support for women's colleges and for continuing education programs for women, a comprehensive report on the state of women in higher education from the Commission on Higher Education, and more – I am convinced this is the work that would most gratify your mother and my grandmother, who knew the value of education.

You, I believe, would heartily approve of our ten-year Partnership for Higher Education in Africa, which brought seven foundations together to increase the resources and impact of higher education – especially for women. Thanks to university and graduate fellowships from Carnegie Corporation, thousands of African women and men have graduated and have begun to transform their societies and nations. I am proud to inform you that, following your example, we too have opened windows to new worlds by supporting various libraries in Africa, including the establishment of two national libraries, a children's library, and exemplary circulating libraries in South Africa.

We continually look for new ways to support education at home and abroad. Fifty years ago, the Corporation, together with the Ford Foundation, supported another transformative program, an innovative educational experiment on television called *Sesame Street*. It has had a lasting impact on generations of children around the world. Today, we also invest in education through the Andrew Carnegie Fellows, a highly selective program that supports scholarly research, and through grants to organizations like the Institute of International Education and the Brookings Institution.

The Corporation continues to believe, as you did, that with wealth comes responsibility. While adhering to your ideals, we have not forgotten our duty to manage your legacy and trust. Our sense of responsibility and accountability in our grantmaking was best summed up by one of our earlier trustees, who declared that it was incumbent upon us, and indeed all foundations, to have "glass pockets." We place a high priority on the quality of our investments, assessments, and internal auditing; and transparency is an integral part of our mission. I am proud to inform you that we were the first foundation to provide annual reports to the public.

The first-season cast of *Sesame Street*, which premiered on National Educational Television (NET) on November 10, 1969.

We believe that people should know what resources we possess and how we spend and invest those resources. We have evolved with the times, and as a nonprofit organization know that we have to be accountable and responsible not only to our charter, but to the public as well.

In all of our work, we have acted as laboratories for our nation, helping to test the best of new thinking about national security, science, and educational practices. Like you, we continue to believe that people should be taught to help themselves, and that a good idea should ultimately succeed on its own merits. We nurture ideas and disseminate them, but we don't support them indefinitely. The Corporation has made it a point to acknowledge where we have failed, share what we have learned, and thus prevent others from repeating our mistakes in the future.

Throughout your life, you found significant ways to help people lead better lives, individually and together in their communities. When you came to the United States in 1848, I wonder if you had any inkling how much change you would set in motion. Your generosity transformed the country we both grew to love and call home. Indeed, the United States is the world's leading practitioner of philanthropy. Giving has become a profound part of American culture.

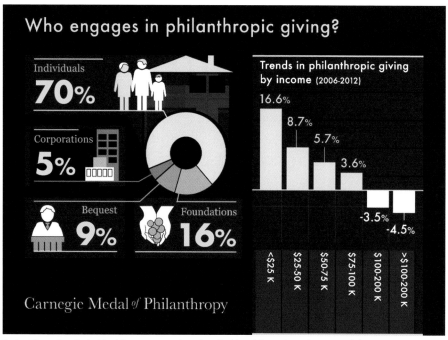

A chart illustrating charitable giving sources and trends in the United States, based on research from organizations such as Giving USA and Philanthropy Roundtable.

Last year, Americans gave over $400 billion, with more than two-thirds of that amount given by people who make less than $75,000 a year. Today, we have more than 1.5 million nonprofit organizations in the United States, supported by the generosity of people throughout the country.

Thanks to the extraordinary work of my colleagues, the Corporation's reach has also grown. From 1911 to 1997, Carnegie Corporation granted one billion dollars. Since 1997, we have given $2.1 billion in grants supporting the work of nonprofit institutions. Today's endowment stands at $3.4 billion.

You taught us that our work is meant to empower others. We constantly strive to do good, by ourselves or in tandem with like-minded organizations. Toward that end, we have increased our cooperation with other foundations. Indeed, when we started our magazine, the *Carnegie Reporter*, we decided to include a few pages highlighting the work of our fellow foundations, as we are all in the realm of philanthropy.

We have also tried to promote the same public-spirited philanthropy that you espoused so well in "The Gospel of Wealth." Since its creation in 2001, the Carnegie Medal of Philanthropy has publicly encouraged a spirit of giving by thanking prominent donors from many different countries. What is more, the Carnegie Medal also led to the revitalization of the Carnegie family of institutions, bettering their collective power and helping them usher in another century of philanthropy devoted to your mission and legacy. I am very proud to inform you that today the Carnegie institutions lift one another up, cooperating with one another to meet the important challenges of our time.

Finally, we share our commitment to your legacy, which continues to touch so many lives. It is a constant pleasure for me to run into people like Justice Thomas who thank me for continuing the work you began. Robert Caro, one of the foremost biographers of our time, told me recently that a grant from Carnegie Corporation enabled him to finish his Pulitzer Prize-winning book *The Power Broker*. The economist Milton Friedman said his life was saved by going to a library you built. In other ways, too, you saved lives — a Carnegie grant resulted in the discovery of insulin for treating diabetes, thus saving millions of lives around the world.

I was once asked if your legacy was a difficult burden to carry. I answered that it would only become a burden if I stopped believing in it. And how could I stop believing in such universal goals? You championed the importance of humanity's welfare, the possibilities of education, the redemptive qualities of science, and the values of a democratic society. Your extraordinary vision still sustains the mission of Carnegie Corporation of New York. Thank you for making your legacy so easy to carry. It has been the privilege of my life to continue your work. I hope this letter will, like the whispers of the "still small voice within," assure you and all future generations that because you lived, "one small part of the great world has been bettered just a little."

Yours,
Vartan Gregorian
President

Carnegie UK Trust

Dear Mr. Carnegie,

I am writing to you from our office on the outskirts of Pittencrieff Park, a view you will have known well during your time in Dunfermline. The park that you bequeathed to the people of your hometown more than a century ago is as beautiful today, on a spring day, as it was then.

It is this view that the staff and trustees of the Carnegie UK Trust see when we come to the office to carry out the duty you bestowed on the organisation, to "improve the wellbeing of the masses," back in 1913. Just out of sight of the office are your statue and the wrought-iron gates, named for Louise Carnegie, at the entrance to the park. The legacy you left behind is built into the fabric of the place where we work.

As with the other institutions that bear your name, you endowed us with many gifts. In addition to the financial endowment of $10 million in steel bonds, your foresight provided two less immediately tangible gifts which have had a lasting impact on the work of the UK Trust.

The first gift was the mission you gave us to improve the wellbeing of people of the UK and Ireland. The scope of wellbeing is unusually wide for a philanthropic organisation. Lord Shaw of Dunfermline, a member of the original Executive Committee, remarked at the time that the vagueness of the deed was terrifying.

The second gift was the faith you placed in the Board of the Trust to interpret what that mission meant. The deed sets out that trustees may "by such means as are embraced within the meaning of the word 'charitable' … from time to time select as best fitted from age to age for securing these purposes, remembering that new needs are constantly arising as the masses advance." Our only restriction, apart from geographical coverage and charitable purposes, is that we must not support war or warlike preparations.

Time has proved these to be two tremendously valuable assets to have been given. By not requiring specific activities, and providing such a general mission statement, you enabled the trustees to adjust their approach over the years, just as you envisioned. The history of the UK can be charted through the work of the Trust. Early twentieth-century concerns around physical welfare gave way to concerns about social welfare. The end of World War II saw economic depression, followed by changing attitudes to women, immigrants, and those with disabilities, and the growing recognition that young people have specific needs in relation to wellbeing. These vast social changes can be seen through the archives of the Trust, as our predecessors analysed the needs of the current population and applied resources accordingly to make improvements.

Your trustees have used varied approaches suited to the time and the issues at hand. Innovative projects included everything from creating the first colleges of adult education, to supporting the first preschool playgroups, and investing in outdoor recreational space for the general population. There are many organisations that would not exist today if you had not endowed the UK Trust with the mission and funds to support their establishment. Charities such as Leonard Cheshire, Citizens Advice Bureaux, Making Music (formerly the National Federation of Music Societies), Sadler's Wells, and the Old Vic were all supported by the Trust. At a more local level, many hundreds of village halls, playing fields, and youth hostels were set up with money from your endowment. UK civil society is all the stronger for them.

When I meet people for the first time and introduce the UK Trust, it is the public libraries you built that people most associate with you. For the first 50 years of our story, more than one third of the funds were allocated to libraries. We moved away from this for a while, focusing on new and emerging areas of need. But rediscovering our connection with libraries, and providing a programme of research and development to support them in the twenty-first century, is one of the things the current team is most proud of. We hope you would also be proud of our continuing commitment to this aspect of your legacy.

Your trustees have never confined themselves to grant giving when interpreting the mission, producing groundbreaking reports on major social issues such as the welfare of mothers and children (1917); the relationship between diet, income, and health (1937); young people's economic opportunities (1943); juvenile delinquency (1950); youth services (1958); the post-war new communities (1960); the arts and disabled people (1981); and rural community development (2004). While we haven't used the words "the masses" for many years, the focus has been firmly on people experiencing disadvantage, and particularly on those whose disadvantage is not well understood by society at the time.

The faith you placed in the trustees allowed them to make a bold decision in 2004 to move from a grant-making to an operating trust. The Trust Deed is interpreted as your ambition to improve conditions for as many people as possible. As the value of the endowment fell, and the UK Trust could no longer claim to be one of the biggest grant-funders in the UK and Ireland, the impact of the grants became smaller and smaller. But the impact of an independent, evidence-based organisation with its focus on improving wellbeing was becoming

The Citizens Advice Bureau was created on the eve of World War II to help people in difficulty, mainly by providing advice on housing, food, and debt.

Established in 1930, the Youth Hostels Association offered young people affordable accommodation in the countryside as an antidote to the harsh conditions of inner-city life.

clear, particularly when we find a new angle from which to explore issues neglected or under-examined by others. And so, today, it is in our capacity as an operating trust that we are able to continue your legacy by influencing policy and practice to improve the lives of people in the UK and Ireland.

Our most recent inquiry of this nature, carried out by Carnegie Fellow Julia Unwin, may surprise you, focusing as it does on kindness. The Trust's involvement in understanding the value and power of kindness is seen as risky and innovative, which may tell you something about the times we are currently living in. And we continue to focus on improving lives directly, tackling complex or challenging issues that our endowment gives us the privilege to dedicate time and resources to when others may find it difficult — such as our support for affordable credit, to ensure that people can access fair credit when they need it most.

Of course, here in 2019, none of the current team in the UK Trust knew you personally. But we have come to know you through the generosity of spirit both in financial terms and in the faith you put in the trustees. We can be inspired by the thought you put into the choice of the word wellbeing — how risky it was at the time, but how forward thinking it has turned out to be.

One of our favourite insights into your character, though, is through your words, "there is little success where there is little laughter." It is with these words that I often finish, when speaking to the organisations we work with. We invariably find that our flexibility and our willingness to focus only on the outcomes for people bring light to those working at the front line of charitable and public services, and joy to our relationships with them.

For that gift, and many, many more, I thank you and extend my gratitude also to all those who came after you, who so carefully stewarded the Trust to achieve its unique mission.

Yours sincerely,
Jennifer Wallace
Interim Joint Chief Executive

Dear Mr. Carnegie,

Not many endeavours survive a century of change, particularly a century of such rapid change as that which has just passed. Your wisdom in giving the trustees your blessing to embrace change has given your UK Trust the freedom not only to survive but to thrive.

For the current trustees, whom I have the present honour to chair, the challenge which we know you would set us is to begin the task of contributing even more to the wellbeing of the people of the British Isles in the next hundred years than we have done in the past one hundred years. It is a big challenge, but one lesson we take from your life is that with sustained ambition and commitment it is possible to achieve more than others, or even we ourselves, might deem possible.

In seeking increased impact on the wellbeing of the mass of people, we are in a position to learn from what has not changed during a century when governments and many others, including us, have sought to bring about improved wellbeing. There has been enormous progress in the prosperity of our society, and in the availability of educational opportunity and medical provision for almost everyone in the British Isles. Yet we can see clearly that the evidence of these many decades of progress is that a large number of people within society derive much less benefit from that progress than the majority.

The people within society who benefit least from general progress would have been recognisable to you in your lifetime. They are those who have to overcome the deficit disadvantages birth and family circumstances have imposed

There has been enormous progress in the prosperity of our society … Yet we can see clearly that the evidence of these many decades of progress is that a large number of people within society derive much less benefit from that progress than the majority.

upon them, before they can participate in the general uplift in wellbeing which others in society are able to enjoy from childhood onwards. For many, the deficit crushes their self belief and belief in the possibility of improvement before they come anywhere close to sharing in the opportunities embraced by others in society.

A development which might be much more surprising to you is that we in the nations of the British Isles, in common with many other economically developed countries, now live in the first human society in history in which the majority of the population is over age 50. In your own lifetime, that was the average age of death in Britain, even as late as the first decade of the twentieth century. In contrast to issues affecting the poorest in society, the challenge of learning to adapt to a society characterised by advanced age is more strongly correlated with those who have enjoyed relative prosperity in their earlier adult lives.

At one stage of recent thinking, discussions of both sets of issues – the persistence of relative poverty and the need to adapt to increased ageing – were interwoven with discussion of the increased importance of a supply of skilled labour in the most developed economies. More recently, however, debate about the future of work, and the possibility of substantially reduced demand for labour, is emerging as a result of rapid technological advancement through the potential applications of artificial intelligence. We are only beginning to speculate about the nature of a society in which an increasing proportion of people may need to find their sense of value and meaning in ways separate from the contribution they make to the wellbeing of society through work.

As we grapple with the challenge of contributing to the wellbeing of the mass of people by exploring fresh ways of responding positively to the development of our society, we retain continuity with ways of thinking which characterised your own philanthropy.

We advocate the practical value that can come from emulating your focus on general wellbeing as a guiding principle, and we seek to be at the forefront of international thinking about ways governments apply that principle.

We explore ways in which the capacity of individuals, families, and communities can be given greater expression and acknowledgement. We look at the enhancement of wellbeing that can come from the ways in which people cooperate with one another, and the degree of responsibility we take for the wellbeing of one another, including the ways in which we behave towards one another in everyday life.

We maintain a distinctive focus on understanding and learning from the experience of life in towns throughout the British Isles, assisted both by your decision to ensure that representation from Dunfermline, the town of your birth, is a substantial component of our trustee group, and by our continued location in the town.

We shall continue to learn from you, and from the perspectives you bequeathed to us, as we strive to live up to the trust you have invested in us, and in our successors as trustees in the century ahead, to take forward your legacy of philanthropy. You gave us the responsibility to reinterpret the ways in which we can best give effect to your intentions in the light of changing times, and we shall continue to embrace that responsibility wholeheartedly.

With our gratitude and respect,
Sir John Elvidge
Chair, Board of Trustees

Carnegie Council for Ethics in International Affairs

Dear Mr. Carnegie,

As the current president of the Carnegie Council for Ethics in International Affairs, it is my privilege to report to you on the eve of the 100th anniversary of our founding.

It is not often that we have an opportunity to think in terms of 100 years. It's a span well-suited to remind us that while our lives are time-bound, our connections endure. And as much as things change, they remain the same.

Looking back in a personal way, I can see and feel your world of 1914. I can imagine my grandfather, soon to be a telegraph officer in the U.S. Army, his tour of duty awaiting him in France. Today, I find myself wondering if his Morse code was really much different than our texts and Twitter — all dots and dashes turned into hashtags and pixels. Looking forward, I can almost visualize our successors in 2114. I suspect that whatever technology they use to communicate 100 years from now, it will be both simple and astounding — in some ways familiar enough for us to understand, and in other ways astonishing. As much as things change, they remain the same.

Carnegie Council for Ethics in International Affairs remains proud to be the youngest of your endowments — the last one you established. We remember you created us with urgency just prior to the outbreak of the war. As I understand it, your animating idea for yet another Carnegie initiative was the belief that politics was not just the business of institution building, it was also the business of moral transformation. It was not enough to build the Peace Palace at The Hague and to lobby kaisers, kings, tsars, and presidents to establish the League of Nations and World Court. Peaceful resolution of conflict would depend on changing patterns of behavior, and this change would depend, ultimately, on moral arguments and educational efforts in favor of peace.

The challenge for us today, as it was at the time of our founding, is to use our moral traditions to help us imagine a better future. Today's Carnegie Council focuses on the one central question that preoccupied you and your colleagues at our founding: How can we learn to live together peacefully while acknowledging our deepest differences?

The history of the past 100 years shows that in your assessment of world politics, you got some things right, others wrong. This is the all-important background upon which our Council has tried to make its mark on the world. Let's start with what you got right.

You were perhaps most right about the stubborn nature of militarism. We know now that the glorification of war in 1914 led to "the trenches, the mud, the rats, the typhus, and the general futility of World War I" [a quote from Nicholson Baker's essay, "Why I'm a Pacifist"] and the wars that followed. It is only with tragic irony today that we quote the poet's *Dulce et decorum est pro patria mori* — how sweet and right it is to die for one's country. Even the bitterness of World War I did not stem the numerous twentieth-century slaughters that followed. And yet, despite all of the blood spilled, can we say that the glorification of war has receded?

You were also right about the corrosive effects of imperialism. Your offer to pay $20 million to purchase the Philippine Islands in order to insure their independence was a gesture as heartfelt as it was dramatic. As you said at the time, it is neither natural nor morally right for powerful nations to rule over the less powerful. Empire saps the dignity of both the rulers and the ruled. The past 100 years show that empire bears its share of responsibility for the sorry record of rivalry and conflict in the twentieth century. Many of the political struggles we see today, particularly in the Middle East, can be traced directly to the redrawing of maps in 1919. Economic struggle — especially the persistence of vast global economic inequality — also must be considered in this light.

Photograph and dedication from Andrew Carnegie to The Church Peace Union — the original name of the Carnegie Council for Ethics in International Affairs.

A statement of sympathy from The Church Peace Union on the death of Andrew Carnegie, recalling his "unfailing, loyal, and enthusiastic devotion" to peace.

You were right about the centrality of self-determination and minority rights as keystones to living in a peaceful world. In a world of divided communities, peace depends on pluralism. Pluralism demands institutional arrangements that allow people to live deeply rooted in their communities and yet peaceably with outsiders. Post-World War II Europe has provided a positive example of what is possible. As we see in Scotland today, pluralism is evolving as a peaceful and invigorating concept. But of course this is not so in many other places around the world where pluralism is indeed failing miserably. Over the past 100 years we have learned we should not underestimate the possibilities and the limits of pluralism.

Finally, you were right about the stubborn nature of religion as a formative element in both war and peace. Religion has surely played its role in conflicts — sometimes exacerbated by leaders who have self-righteously and cynically used religious ideology and moral rhetoric to pursue their interests. Yet religiously inspired voices have also been central to the promotion of human dignity and social justice. In either case, we live in a world today that is still often defined according to religious principles in contest.

Let's turn for a moment to what you got wrong. You were wrong about the simple allure of peace — the assumption that citizens and leaders will inevitably value peace as the highest good. As Kenneth Roth, executive director of Human Rights Watch, said recently when asked for a comment on the use of chemical weapons in Syria: "War is obviously terrible, but it's not the ultimate evil. Some things are worse, and one is the deliberate slaughter of civilians." Or as Barack Obama put it in his Nobel Lecture, "Evil does exist in the world. A nonviolent movement could not have halted Hitler's armies. Negotiations cannot convince al Qaeda's leaders to lay down their arms. To say that force may sometimes be necessary is not a call to cynicism — it is recognition of history; the imperfections of man, and the limits of reason."

In this vein, you were also wrong about the presumed strength of law as the ultimate trump to power politics. Law depends on both reason and reciprocity, two qualities not always in great supply, especially in extreme situations. The force of reason rarely trumps the imperatives of necessity, realpolitik, ideology, or national mythologies.

You were wrong to assume that international institutions like the League of Nations could temper the heat of national ambitions and shape cold calculations of national interests. For all the moderating influences of international institutions, the Great Powers would never respond faithfully to distant, faceless, unaccountable bureaucracies. Rather, the Great Powers would tend to use such organizations as instruments of power — as a means rather than an end to international politics. As many American secretaries of state have said in commenting upon the United Nations, our approach is "together where we can, alone where we must."

Finally, you were wrong about the inevitability of social progress. What your biographers have called your cockeyed optimism fed your liberal illusion that peace was merely a technical matter — something that could be engineered by societies that were becoming ever more civilized with the passing of time.

As you demonstrated with all of your philanthropy, it is indeed possible to change the way people think. It is indeed possible to change what is considered moral, just, and right. Legitimacy rests on sentiment and judgment. Legitimacy is, ultimately, a matter of human decision.

Your favorite saying, "All is well since all grows better," may have reflected your personal experience. But today we have to face the fact that we live in a split world. There are haves and have-nots, those who live in zones of peace while others live in zones of conflict. For those of us in the privileged world, things are indeed good. For at least two billion of our brothers and sisters in poor and unstable areas, things are not so good, and there is no presumption of good times ahead.

For all you got wrong, however, there is an undeniable opportunity we have to build on your legacy to shape the future and to work for positive change. And this is what I would like to focus on in this last section of my report. As you demonstrated with all of your philanthropy, it is indeed possible to change the way people think. It is indeed possible to change what is considered moral, just, and right. Legitimacy rests on sentiment and judgment. Legitimacy is, ultimately, a matter of human decision.

You were persistent in pointing out that civilized nations abandoned practices like slavery and dueling. Surely, you thought, the practice of war — the killing of man by man — would follow into extinction. You would be pleased to know that Steven Pinker wrote a book last year (*The Better Angels of our Nature*) arguing that while war is still too much with us, the world is indeed a less violent place than it was 100 years ago. Following your line of thought, he argued that this trend toward a less violent world is inextricably bound to a shift in ethics — a shift in what is considered expected and required behavior.

We have learned over the past 100 years that ethics matter. And here is where our Council has tried to do its part. Ethics, as we practice it, goes beyond moral assertion to entertain competing moral claims. For us, ethics invites moral argument rather than moral assertion. Ethical inquiry enables us to include all moral arguments, religious and secular. It gives equal moral voice to all while giving us the tools to think for ourselves and stand our ground accordingly.

We like to think of our approach today as a sort of enlightened realism — a realism that enables us to understand our own values and interests in light of the values and interests of others. This approach demands the humility to abandon any hint of a crusading spirit and a genuine commitment to try to understand the point of view of others. This is the intent and purpose of our Centennial project, built on hard-won lessons of historical experience, pluralist and pragmatic in nature.

Thanks to the rapid expansion and advances of communications technology, it is now possible for the Carnegie Council to encourage a multi-directional global conversation. Our Studio and Global Ethics Network ventures leverage advances in digital media in service of the enduring values that have guided the Council through its history. We convene, publish, and broadcast programs that reach hundreds of thousands of people around the world. We believe we are honoring your intention to imagine a better future — together with our viewers, listeners, and readers — through education and advocacy for ethics.

None of this is done alone. The value of an institution like Carnegie Council for Ethics in International Affairs is its ability to transmit values over time and space through the lives of the people it touches. So the work continues. We have been very lucky in friendship — especially in the relationships we have developed around the world. I trust that 100 years from now, our successors will have such strong voices for ethics at their side to keep alive the idea that peace is indeed worth fighting for.

Sincerely,
Joel H. Rosenthal
President

This talk, given in 2014 at the Scottish Parliament in Edinburgh, at the Carnegie Council Centennial Symposium entitled "From World War to a Global Ethic," inspired this collection of letters to Andrew Carnegie on the centenary of his death.

TIAA

TEACHERS INSURANCE AND ANNUITY ASSOCIATION OF AMERICA

Dear Mr. Carnegie,

More than a century ago, you had a groundbreaking vision for how to provide a financially secure retirement to some of society's most deserving workers. TIAA was the result. I think you'd be gratified to see how your ideas have not only endured, but flourished. Thanks to your generosity and foresight, TIAA has helped make a secure retirement possible for generations of people who, like you, have made a difference in the world.

TIAA recently celebrated our centennial, which gave us many opportunities to tell the inspirational story of our founding. That story began when you joined Cornell University's board of trustees in 1890 and were shocked to learn how paltry professors' salaries were. Given your great admiration for educators, it pained you to see that they had to either retire to lives of poverty or keep working well into their old age. You were determined to "remove a source of deep and constant anxiety to the poorest paid and yet one of the highest of all professions," which you also knew would help strengthen the American higher education system.

Your unprecedented $10 million donation in 1905 to create a "free pension" system for professors, which required no contributions from employer or employee, worked so well that it quickly became clear it was unsustainable. By creating the Teachers Insurance and Annuity Association in 1918 with a $1 million grant from Carnegie Corporation of New York, you delivered the long-term answer to higher ed's retirement challenge.

Most importantly, because of you, millions of people have been able to pursue careers that enable them to make the world a better place, comfortable in the knowledge that they can retire in financial security when their work is done.

Predating the establishment of the U.S. Social Security system, TIAA was a true innovation, built on what was then a revolutionary concept: providing participants with individually owned, contractual, contributory, fully funded annuities under an employer-sponsored retirement plan. This new model was voluntary, and it placed the responsibility of saving for retirement on both employers and employees; portability was a key element of its design, enabling participants to keep their savings even when they switched jobs.

The TIAA model, which was eventually extended from higher education to workers in the broader not-for-profit community, has been, by any measure, a huge success. In our first 100 years, we've provided $459 billion in annuity payments and other benefits to our participants. We've never missed a payment, even through the depressions, recessions, wars, market crashes, and other crises that marked the past century.

Certainly, TIAA has not remained static since our founding. We've carried your spirit of innovation throughout our history, evolving to keep pace with the changing needs of the people and institutions we serve. One of the most monumental changes came in 1952, when the legendary William C. Greenough, whom some have called the second father of TIAA, led the team that created an entirely new kind of investment — the variable annuity. This gave participants access to the stock market and its higher expected returns, and proved to be a critically important addition to the fixed-income investments on which TIAA was built. Like you, Greenough was solving a problem that threatened retirement security. But in this case, the challenge was rising inflation, which was ravaging the purchasing power of the dollar and taking a toll on retirees trying to stretch a fixed and limited income over increasing expenses.

Today, owning stocks is taken for granted as a core part of achieving retirement security, but it was a real departure from the common wisdom of the time. A *Fortune* magazine editor described Greenough's creation — the College Retirement Equities Fund, or CREF — as "the biggest development in the insurance/investment business since the passage of the Social Security Act." We became known as TIAA-CREF until 2016, when we decided to simplify by returning to the name you originally gave us.

TIAA has innovated in many other ways through the years in the pursuit of retirement security for our participants. In the 1970s, we were one of the first companies to use an extensive portfolio of international stocks as part of our investment strategy. In 1995, we created the TIAA Real Estate Account, giving our participants the opportunity to invest in directly owned real estate properties. More recently, we began investing in alternative assets such as farmland, timberland, and energy, thanks in part to the wise guidance of former TIAA Trustee David Swensen and others. While we now have many more tools in our toolbox than we did in 1918, the goal remains the same: financial wellbeing for the people and institutions we serve.

I think you might be surprised by how much TIAA has grown over the years. By the end of our first year of existence, we had about $1 million in assets and served 30 institutional clients and 464 individuals with three full-time employees. By the end of our first century, we had become a Fortune 100 company with more than $1 trillion in assets under management and administration, serving more than 15,000 institutional clients and 5 million individual clients,

The TIAA Bank building in Jacksonville, Florida, headquarters for the comprehensive banking services TIAA began offering customers in 2018.

A graphic aimed at TIAA professionals encourages making a difference for customers, company, and community.

with more than 17,500 employees in 375 offices in 24 countries. We remained the leading retirement provider in higher ed and the broader not-for-profit retirement market. We had become the world's largest agricultural investor and one of the top five commercial real estate managers.

In recent years, we have expanded our capabilities and broadened the range of products and services we offer. We recognize that getting people to and through a financially secure retirement means addressing their financial needs and helping them build financial wellness throughout all the stages of their lives. We are now providing banking services through our TIAA Bank. We provide financial advice to our clients in many different ways. We are building a global asset management business under the Nuveen brand name to drive the long-term performance that delivers outstanding outcomes to our clients. We're taking bold steps to ensure that we continue to be as successful in our second century as we've been in our first. Our clients are counting on us for that.

You might be disappointed to know that the retirement challenge you identified — and solved — so long ago continues to persist in many other areas of society. In fact, some are predicting a retirement crisis in the United States due to the convergence of a number of forces: the shift away from defined benefit plans in the private sector, a lack of adequate savings by Americans, and increasing lifespans that will mean many more years in retirement than in previous generations. We believe a key way to address these twenty-first-century challenges is the same solution you hit upon in the last century: translating retirement savings into guaranteed lifetime income. Your idea may have been radical in 1918, but it's clear that it's worked beautifully, and it's every bit as relevant today as it was then. We are doing all we can to make sure the benefits of lifetime income — and the value of the TIAA model — are widely known.

In closing, I want to thank you, Mr. Carnegie, on behalf of all of us who love TIAA and its mission. In creating TIAA, you transformed retirement in higher education, as you set out to do, but the impact has been far greater than you could have imagined. Most importantly, because of you, millions of people have been able to pursue careers that enable them to make the world a better place, comfortable in the knowledge that they can retire in financial security when their work is done. Your legacy has endured in their lives and contributions, and in the lives of all who have been touched by their work. It will continue to endure in the lives of all those TIAA will serve in our second century — and beyond.

Roger Ferguson
President and Chief Executive Officer

Carnegie Family

Dear Grandpa Neigie,

Thank you for your letter. I am glad you enjoyed all the family news. You asked how things were going generally with the Carnegie legacy, and I will try to give you a rough overview.

First of all, out of your foundations existing in 1919, all bar two are thriving today. The two no longer with us are the German Hero Fund, which was closed down in 1937, and the French Hero Fund, which in 2011 decided to close and use its endowment to fund a Fulbright scholarship. To prevent further closures, the Hero Fund Commission in Pittsburgh took the initiative to create an umbrella body called the Carnegie Hero Funds World Committee. With funding from Carnegie Corporation of New York, it has been successful in encouraging the remaining Hero Funds, particularly in the cases of Belgium, Switzerland, and Italy. All the Hero Funds depend on the dedication of the individuals who run them and in that regard they have been most fortunate.

One of the changes that has taken place in the last 20 years has been the creation of the Medal of Philanthropy, which is given every two years to those individual philanthropists who follow your example of giving. The involvement of all the Carnegie foundations in the selection process has had the happy consequence of bringing all your foundations together. At the biennial award ceremony, representatives from the Carnegie foundations attend a specially convened business meeting and meet informally during the ceremony events.

On the British front the foundations have been hampered by not being able to grow their endowments as successfully as their American counterparts. This was largely due to the restrictive investment rules imposed on charities over most of the last century and, more recently, less favourable tax rules. Nevertheless, the UK foundations continue to evolve and thrive. They are now all housed together in a single purpose-built office in Pittencrieff Park in Dunfermline. The prize-winning building fits seamlessly into the landscape on the north side of the park.

The one area of your legacy which has not achieved what it set out to achieve is the abolishment of war. Although there has not been a world war for nearly 75 years, there have been plenty of smaller ones. Airborne ordnance has meant civilians continue to bear the brunt of the casualties. There is also a global threat from terrorists who use the random slaughter of unarmed and unprotected civilians to further their aims. The imposing Peace Palace in The Hague has had some success in providing a forum for peaceful resolution of disputes between countries, but nothing done so far has been effective in stopping humans from killing each other.

One of your initiatives which has become obsolete is the funding of church organs. The decline in church attendance in the UK has brought the closure of many churches and therefore there are fewer organs. However, those that remain are usually lovingly maintained and, where applicable, their rich tones continue to relieve the monotony of the sermon.

Libraries are also under threat as the local authority councils struggle to find funding to keep them running. Yet they remain a core part of society, and closures are usually fiercely contested by concerned citizens.

You will be glad to know that your beloved Skibo continues — now as a country club. The castle and grounds are beautifully looked after, and the club provides a lot of local employment in the area. Golf thrives in Dornoch and surrounding areas. The 9-hole ladies course at Dornoch, which Grandma Neigie was instrumental in establishing, has been extended to a full 18-hole course, and the lovely little 9-hole course at Bonar Bridge which she opened in 1904

Your example of giving away your huge fortune has been widely adopted by others, and the name Carnegie is synonymous with philanthropy. We, your descendants, are immensely proud of you — your great reputation is the best inheritance ever.

remains as popular as ever. The Carnegie Shield, reputed to be one of golf's most valuable trophies, is keenly contested every year, and this year it will be for the 106th time.

Your family continues to grow. From your single offspring, Margaret, born in 1898, came four grandchildren and from them 14 great-grandchildren. Then came 32 great, great-grandchildren and now great, great, great-grandchildren are beginning to arrive.

In summary, I would say that all is well with the Carnegie legacy. Your foundations, which you wisely left unfettered by restrictive rules, have adapted well to the changing world. Their work has helped to improve the lives of hundreds of thousands, perhaps millions, of individuals. Your example of giving away your huge fortune has been widely adopted by others, and the name Carnegie is synonymous with philanthropy. We, your descendants, are immensely proud of you — your great reputation is the best inheritance ever.

William
William Thomson, CBE
Chairman Emeritus, Carnegie UK Trust

ACKNOWLEDGMENTS

In *Letters to Andrew Carnegie*, members of the Carnegie family of institutions reflect on the character and intentions of our founder, and examine how a century of our collective effort measures up to his aspirations. Reading these letters makes clear what a transformational visionary Andrew Carnegie was, and how lasting is his influence. This collection would have been impossible without the valuable contributions of our colleagues, and we acknowledge and thank them all.

Credits

Page 8, illustration courtesy of Carnegie Hall Archives. **Page 9**, photograph by Jeff Goldberg.
Page 11, photographs by Chris Lee. **Pages 14 and 16**, photographs courtesy of Carnegie Library of Pittsburgh.
Pages 19–25, photographs courtesy of Carnegie Museums of Pittsburgh. **Pages 27–32**, photographs
provided courtesy of Carnegie Mellon University. **Pages 36 and 39**, photographs courtesy of Carnegie Trust
for the Universities of Scotland. **Pages 41 and 45**, photographs courtesy of Carnegie Institution for Science.
Page 46, left, photograph courtesy of Desert Botanical Laboratory Papers, University of Arizona Library Special
Collections; right, photograph courtesy of Carnegie Institution for Science. **Page 50**, illustration courtesy of
Peace Palace. **Page 54**, photograph by Arjan de Jager. **Page 59**, photographs courtesy of Carnegie Hero Fund
Commission. **Pages 62–65**, photographs courtesy of Carnegie Dunfermline and Hero Fund Trusts.
Page 68, photograph courtesy of Carnegie Rescuers Foundation (Switzerland). **Page 69**, photograph courtesy
of Aargauer Zeitung; photographer: Tobias Hänni. **Page 83**, photograph courtesy of Stichting Carnegie
Heldenfonds. **Pages 90 and 91**, photographs courtesy of Carnegie Foundation for the Advancement of Teaching.
Pages 94 and 95, photographs courtesy of Carnegie Endowment for International Peace. **Page 102**, photograph
by Alex Wong/Getty Images. **Page 105**, photographer: Charlotte Brooks, LOOK Magazine Collection, Library
of Congress, Prints & Photographs Division. **Page 106**, infographic courtesy of Carnegie Corporation of New York.
Page 111, photographs courtesy of Carnegie UK Trust. **Page 119**, photographs courtesy of Carnegie Council for
Ethics in International Affairs. **Page 128**, left, photograph courtesy of TIAA Bank; right, infographic courtesy of TIAA.

Editor: Karen Theroux
Designer: James McKibben

CORPORATION
OF NEW YORK